THE SUNDAY TIMES BOOK OF
PERSONAL
FINANCE

THE SUNDAY TIMES BOOK OF
PERSONAL
FINANCE

Edited by Diana Wright

A Graham Tarrant Book

David & Charles
Newton Abbot London North Pomfret (Vt)

British Library Cataloguing in Publication Data
The Sunday Times book of personal finance
1. Personal finance. Manuals
I. Wright, Diana
332.024

ISBN 0-7153-9111-9
ISBN 0-7153-9220-4 Pbk

Phototypeset by Typesetters (Birmingham) Ltd
and printed in Great Britain
by Billings & Son Ltd, Worcester
for David & Charles Publishers plc
Brunel House Newton Abbot Devon

Distributed in the United States of America
by David & Charles Inc
North Pomfret Vermont 05053 USA

Contents

Introduction

Money affects everybody - for good or bad. Whether you unashamedly love it or whether you have a sneaking suspicion that you spend too long thinking about it, this book is for you; in fact particularly if you belong to the latter class. The trouble with money is that, often, the less you want to think about it, the more you are forced to, as money worries and financial problems rear their ugly head.

What this book won't attempt to tell you, let me make clear at the start, is how to Get Rich. There's no secret to that, any more than there's a secret 'miracle diet' which will burn off the pounds while letting you eat everything you want.

The 'secret' of getting rich is a simple matter of picking the share that doubles over a few weeks, or buying premium bonds that win the top prize, or then again, perhaps you could discover the secret of alchemy or devise a product that everyone will want at any price, and that only you can provide.

And that is all there is to it? There's no real secret? What a disappointment! How boring! you may say. And how wrong you would be: it's not half as boring as struggling to make ends meet on an inadequate pension, as paying out large sums in tax which you could so easily have spent on more enjoyable things, or trying to sort out the priorities from a tangled web of creditors.

And while I accept you may not find the intricacies of life assurance as interesting as I do, or the workings of the stock market a source of such constant fascination as Simon Rose clearly does, or indeed the maze of pensions opportunities such an enjoyable topic of conversation as Adrian Waddingham – to name three of the writers of the following chapters – you will, I hope, find the book interesting and useful, if not in the 'miracle' category.

Only two sorts of people have absolutely no problems with money. Paupers – and the very, *very* rich. In between come probably 99 per cent of the population, which gives plenty of room for error in describing the 'typical investor'.

Even such an apparently straightforward exercise as deciding how much of your assets should be set aside in an 'emergency kitty' becomes practically impossible: speaking from bitter experience, I would suggest that anyone living in a Victorian home, whose 'original features' include the roof, plumbing and indigenous damp, should go for a kitty whose dimensions match those wonderfully high ceilinged (but so expensive to heat) reception rooms.

Others, I know, will brush that aside. 'That's nothing! You should try putting two – three – four children through private schools, *and* with university to follow'. Oh, says a third, you think that's difficult? You should try giving up your job, where your salary is more-or-less index linked (and probably a great deal more); you should try living on my pension and my investments, where any increase I get is dependent on the vagaries of interest rates, the generosity of the pension scheme trustees and the capacity of those companies I've invested in to earn decent profits.

Few people genuinely desire money for its own sake; it's what it can do that is important. Equally, however, I have met few people whose money outstrips their ideas as to what to do with it. Nevertheless, their ideas will be vastly different according to what those railway-obsessed Victorians called their station in life – then, a euphemism for how rich or poor you were, but it could be just as appropriately used to describe where you are in the various stages of life.

Depending on that, some of the chapters in this book may have little or no relevance for you; if you are retired, for instance, you may not be much interested in how you could have organised your pension planning; while the father struggling with a school fees problem would not be directly interested in how to swing round his savings to cope with the different needs of retirement compared to an earning life.

The authors of the book are all regular contributors to *The Sunday Times Personal Finance* pages, and many have a more direct experience of their subjects than simply writing about them. Tony Hetherington, who takes us through the financial staging posts of life in Chapter One, gleaned an intimate knowledge of people's financial planning problems from some years spent working in the gamekeeper's hut of the Inland Revenue; Simon Rose, who writes on the Stock Exchange in Chapter Four, cut his teeth working for a major firm of London stockbrokers before leaving to become a full-time writer and broadcaster.

Raymond Godfrey, a Fellow of the Institute of Taxation, is the author of Chapter Six on school fees planning, and fits in his writing between running a financial publications company and advisory work on tax planning; he has advised many individuals on their own school fees planning. Adrian Waddingham is the writer on pensions, and is an actuary who worked as an adviser to several large companies on their pension schemes before setting up his own independent consultancy.

Joe Irving, who writes on the financial considerations of retirement in Chapter Nine, himself 'retired' from the *Sunday Times* financial pages a few years ago, only to find (as so often happens) that he is busier than ever, contributing to a large number of papers and specialist magazines.

Whatever your financial situation, getting to grips with cash flow is an essential part of planning, and Chapter Two – Nest Eggs and Cash Flow – should provide all the information (not to mention inspiration) to succeed. Chapter Three deals with your home and mortgage. As competition hots up between lenders, there's a greater than ever choice on how to finance the purchase of your house, and given that a mortgage is one of those financial facts of life that stay around for many years to come, it is important to make a proper choice.

Chapters Four and Five bite the bullet of equity investment – buying stocks and shares. Chapter Four, as mentioned earlier, concerns the direct buying of shares; Chapter Five by Peter Fuller, a financial journalist, is about 'pooled investments' where your money is bundled together with others' to buy a wider spread of shares than you could probably afford on your own.

Logic and experience both support the theory that risk and reward are inextricably linked. It is only by investing in 'real' things such as businesses and property that you stand a decent chance of seeing your capital grow in real terms. But there is risk involved, and everyone should think carefully before deciding how much, if any, of their capital they should use in this way.

Writing in early 1988, with the thud of the October '87 stock market crash still ringing in our ears, it is perhaps unnecessary to labour too much the point about risk. Certainly, if you are constitutionally averse to taking risks, if the idea genuinely keeps you awake at nights, you should stick to building societies, or perhaps bank deposits or National Savings.

In the heady days before the crash, when every unit trust seemed to put on 50 per cent a year, and when every privatisation meant a double-your-money game, it seemed like a time when everybody had not only an opportunity but practically a duty to get rich by dabbling in the stock market.

That's nonsense, of course; you don't have to take risks you don't want to, though you should probably be grateful that your pension scheme managers, and the investment experts behind your endowment policy, take a different point of view. But for their willingness to invest in equities on your behalf, you'd stand precious little chance of enjoying an adequate pension, or being able to pay off your mortgage at the end of the day.

On the other side of the coin are people who are all too willing to take risks. Many of the readers' letters which pour into *The Sunday Times* each week relate to problems with equity investment, where someone has believed too readily a salesman's tale.

Although financial planning should be tailored to the needs of the individual, the general order of priorities applies to just about everyone: one, try to keep a sensible sum aside for emergencies; two, make sure you have adequate life assurance to protect your dependants should you die; three, check your pension arrangements so that you will have enough to live on when you retire.

Thereafter, it's an open field, and much depends on your personal preferences and circumstances. At every stage in the game, sadly, the question of tax rears its ugly head. If you are sensible, you will adjust your tactics to make sure your investments are as tax efficient as can be; but you will not let the matter of tax dictate your overall strategy. Just remember that the most tax efficient way of going about things is to spend your way through your capital (no income tax) and make losses on what's left, which solves the problem of Capital Gains Tax and Inheritance Tax at a stroke!

But despite the avowed aim of the Chancellor, the investment playing field is still full of molehills, and the different vehicles that you can use for investment can have a marked effect on the end result. Chapter Ten

highlights the impact of tax and how to build it into financial planning.

This book cannot take the place of professional advice or
– if you prefer to run your own financial ship – personal
legwork and research. Economic and stock market conditions
change - taxation changes – interest rates move up or down.
But how do you go about finding such advice, and what
standards of advice should you expect from those who offer
it? Chapter Eleven by Richard Woods outlines the scope of
the Financial Services Act, which is due to become effective
in stages throughout 1988, and which should set better overall
standards throughout the whole financial industry.

Law and practice do not always coincide, however, and
the chapter contains essential pointers to how (and when)
you should complain if things go wrong. It also suggests how
to go about finding a good financial adviser. Unfortunately,
there is no simple answer to this, any more than there is to
the question 'which is the best share to put my money in?'
Only hindsight will give us the answer to that, and the best
tools we have to play with are background knowledge and
good judgement.

The aim of the contributors to this book is to give you a
helping of each – and to wish you good luck!

Diana Wright

1 The Seven Ages of Financial Man

There are, according to William Shakespeare, seven ages of man, and it is in many ways a convenient fiction to think that we can today divide our lives up into neat little compartments, each with its own set of financial priorities.

But the Bard of Avon lived some time before the arrival of credit cards, cheque books, life assurance, and privatisation (or nationalisation, for that matter!). And man's progress in *As You Like It* from infancy through to second childhood via a career in the army ('full of strange oaths') and as a justice ('full of wise saws') will hardly have universal application nowadays as far as men are concerned, let alone women – but then Shakespeare's female characters did not, for the most part, have careers and money of their own anyway.

Today, whether life can be segmented or not, financial planning without a doubt comes under the heading of 'cradle to grave' strategy, beginning at birth.

Most babies receive gifts, often of cash, which parents may or may not spend instantly on a bumper supply of all the equipment needed to support the new arrival. If they decide to save the cash, the question arises of where to put it. In many ways the decision hinges on the same issues as if the investment was being made by an adult, for an adult. For how long should the money be tied up? What security is there? Is interest taxed at source more convenient and sensible than interest paid gross?

Even the source of the money makes a difference: interest on cash given to an infant by its parent is counted as the parent's income for tax purposes, except for a rather token £5 a year to which the tax man turns a blind eye; interest on money given by other relatives or friends is treated by the tax man as belonging to the child. So, either spend parental gifts of money or invest for growth, with a minimum of income. But consider investing cash from others in, for example, a National Savings investment account or income bond, interest on which is paid gross and will not, in practice, be taxed except in the very rare circumstance of a child whose income exceeds the single person's tax allowance – and not many infant investors manage this!

There are one or two other pitfalls to watch out for as well. A whole range of investments, including savings certificates and most bank deposit accounts, will accept money in a child's own name from the moment it is born – but will not normally allow withdrawals until the child is seven years old.

There is some flexibility in this rule. The Department for National Savings, for example, would not stand in the way of a parent's request that a child's money be moved from one issue of savings certificate to another, higher-paying issue. But plans to withdraw money simply to spend it on non-essentials might well be vetoed, so parents should be aware that some investments really will take care of their child's money – and will do so for seven years, whether they like it or not!

If private education is something you aim for, it is never too soon to start planning, though the amount of planning you can do may be dictated by the amount of money available from you or other members of your family. There are many school fees schemes available, but remember, it is up to you to decide what level of spending you want to go for. These schemes do not guarantee to pay specific school fees, but to generate sums of money at the times you have decided they will be needed.

They are divided into two sorts: income schemes and capital schemes.

In the first, you will typically be asked to pay regular premiums over a period of years. The money goes into a series of life policies which mature one after the other, as cash is needed to pay fees. Naturally, as soon as the first policy matures the premiums start to decrease, leaving you with more spendable income of your own.

Capital schemes involve putting down a lump sum as many years as possible in advance of needing money for school fees. The money is invested, often in a deferred annuity which begins to pay benefits just as the child begins his or her education.

Some schools also offer their own schemes in which payment can be made in advance. The school then invests the money. And if your decision on private education has been left to the last moment, all is not lost. Many insurance brokers and banks (National Westminster, for example) offer loan schemes specifically to cover school fees.

Until the 1988 Budget it was possible to build into a school fees plan a deed of covenant in favour of the child, usually from a grandparent or some other relative. Covenants are still legal but now they are no more than the formalising of a promise to pay a regular sum to someone for a predetermined minimum period. The tax advantages have disappeared except for pre-Budget deeds. They will continue working their tax magic until they expire.

Perhaps the nearest thing still possible is a deed of settlement. The donor will transfer shares, property, or a sum of money, to trustees to invest for the child's benefit. Income from the trust fund can be used towards school fees or for any other purpose, and it will count as the child's income for tax purposes.

If, as is likely, the child does not have sufficient income to warrant tax being due, the parents can reclaim on the child's behalf any tax already paid by the trustees or which has been deducted from trust income such as dividends.

Two notes of warning, however. Firstly, an old-style deed of covenant meant the donor handed over a slice of his or her income. Under a deed of settlement the donor will part with capital savings forever, and if the plan is to generate income for the beneficiary then the capital sum needed will have to be fairly big for the plan to be worthwhile.

And secondly, parents cannot gain any tax advantage from executing a deed of settlement in favour of their own child, nor can they 'swap' children with a friend or neighbour, each benefiting the other's child. As with covenants, grandparents are the most likely candidates to be pressed into executing a deed of settlement.

As children grow older their income will, in the normal run of things, rise. But savings decisions are still mainly based on the same criteria at, say, eleven, as at age one.

The difference is that as they grow older children can be encouraged to make up their own minds as to what offers the best value. The building society offering a free magazine or even a more expensive gift when you open an account may not, in the long run, offer a better return than the bank which offers nothing other than interest – or vice versa. The child who learns to keep his or her eye on the financial return and not be distracted will leave school one step ahead of the child still mesmerised by fringe benefits.

Starting work is a milestone in anyone's life, and in more ways than one. The hours are probably longer than those at school or university – but you do get paid, of course!

At this stage it is time to broaden your horizons. You should have a current account at a major bank. A deposit account does no harm but is far from essential, though you might find evidence of saving useful if you think you might want a mortgage from your bank someday.

Hedging your bets, a building society account makes sense for exactly the same reason. You might even have two accounts – one for regular saving, which should earn you a bit more interest than the basic yield, and another for instantly available cash.

Start thinking about branching out into unit trusts too. Unless you are the sort of precocious brat who has been flipping through the pages of the *Financial Times* since you were eight, unit trusts will introduce you to The City, stocks and shares, dividends, and the whole concept of an investment which can fall in value as well as rise – an education in itself.

In recent years it has been easy to make a profit of 50 per cent on a unit trust within twelve months. It has not even been unusual to make 75 per cent or 100 per cent. But as many investors discovered in October 1987, the small print in unit trust advertisements warning that prices can fall as well as rise is not there for decorative purposes. So, tread carefully, do not commit more than you can afford, and do not lose sleep if prices move down instead of up. If you are a worrier, steer clear.

Unit trusts spread your money around various shares, and the fund managers decide what to buy and sell, and when. Many investors move on to buy individual company shares for themselves, but this only makes sense if you are prepared to spend time taking an interest in the City pages of the daily press – or if you trust your stockbroker or other adviser completely. Learn to judge risks before taking them.

Life cover should start to feature in your thinking in your early twenties. The average teenager has little or no need of life insurance, which is to protect dependants, or life assurance, which is both to protect dependants and to provide a lump sum if you survive a predetermined length of time. If you are a teenager and you do have dependants then do by all means consider life cover (term cover is probably the cheapest and best value for you), but otherwise it is something you need not feel guilty about missing out on.

Nevertheless, soon after leaving your teens you should at least be thinking about an endowment policy, the kind of life cover sometimes called a 'savings policy'. This will give you a lump sum in, say, ten, fifteen, or twenty years time – or whatever period you choose. Do not go into this lightly, though. Insurance companies spend most of your first few years' premiums on administrative expenses involved in setting up the policy, including commission paid to the agent who sold it to you. So, if you decide to surrender the policy in its early years, be prepared to be offered only a fraction of what you paid in.

People get married, and divorced, at any age from 16 upwards, and the financial implications vary enormously from age group to age group and from couple to couple, but taking a couple in their mid-twenties, both working, as a typical example, it could well be that financial considerations will steer them away from the altar rather than towards it.

An uninvited spectre at the wedding breakfast in recent years has been the tax inspector. If our young couple are successful Yuppies they could well find their carefully preserved status as basic rate taxpayers goes out of the window as marriage lumps their incomes together and pushes them into the 40 per cent tax bracket. From 1990 the position will change though, as independent taxation for marriage partners is introduced.

There is another current disadvantage to marriage, most keenly felt in the rich south-east of England, and that is that two single people can get two lots of mortgage tax relief whereas a married couple have just one bite at the cherry. So, two singles living together can claim tax relief between them on up to £60,000 in mortgage money, while a married couple is stuck with a £30,000 relief ceiling.

All this changes under the 1988 Budget though. The Chancellor could have made the tax entitlements equal by allowing marriage partners to claim an individual £30,000 slice of mortgage tax relief. Instead he has equalised the score by banning the double tax relief for unwed couples from August 1

– though existing dual-mortgages keep their existing relief.

Whether people marry or not, getting a foot on the property ladder is a Good Thing, as anyone will tell you who has seen the value of their home increase by leaps and bounds in recent years. The profit is largely illusory, of course. It can only be turned into cash by selling the property, and that would be pointless unless you had somewhere else to live. Nevertheless, when you do sell, for whatever reason, any profit made on the sale of your main or only residence is completely tax-free.

But how to get that important first foot on the ladder? There are two main sources of money for house purchase – the banks and the building societies. Both offer straight repayment mortgages in which you repay the loan, with interest, by monthly instalments over a predetermined period, usually between twenty and thirty years.

And both also offer endowment mortgages. With these, your monthly payment goes in two directions: part of it is interest due to the bank or building society on the money they have lent, and part of it goes to a life company as premiums on an endowment policy. When the policy matures it provides a lump sum big enough to pay off the loan in one fell swoop – and hopefully leave a tidy sum over for you as well. If you die during the term of the mortgage then, naturally, the life policy pays off the loan, even if you die just a day after the policy and the mortgage begin.

A straight repayment mortgage may work out cheaper than an endowment mortgage in terms of monthly cash outlay – but remember that if you have dependants you should make sure the mortgage is paid off if anything happens to you. An endowment mortgage includes this automatically, but with a straight repayment mortgage you will need to pay for separate life cover. This is not expensive as the amount of cover you need decreases over the years, in line with the decreasing amount you owe to the bank or building society.

A third way of buying a home is to take out a pension mortgage. This is still very much minority interest stuff, but as the rules governing pensions themselves change, pension mortgages could well grow in popularity. They are similar to an endowment mortgage in that the loan is paid off at the end of the day in one lump sum, by taking cash from your pension fund on retirement, but they do have one big advantage: pension contributions attract tax relief, whereas life assurance premiums do not. Thus, with a pension mortgage you get tax relief on the interest you pay, as usual, and you also get relief on the money you are salting away to pay off the capital.

The average homeowner, according to rather surprising figures from the mortgage lenders, seems to move house about every six years, usually to a more expensive home than the one left behind; so linking home ownership to the whole matter of pension provision might well look increasingly attractive if the pension plan can pay for the house and the house can, in turn, pay for the pension, in a way we shall see shortly.

The laws covering pensions have been the subject of controversy for many years, and anyone who believes the whole area has been in a state of flux for two decades is not imagining it – it's no less than the truth. And 1988 sees yet another upheaval.

In a nutshell, everyone who works, and some people who don't work, pay national insurance contributions which provide a basic state pension on retirement, which happens at 65 for men and 60 for women. Any employee who is not in a company pension plan or something similar is charged extra contributions for an extra pension, but in many cases the same money paid to a private scheme can give better value.

Many people in schemes run by their employer also choose, particularly as retirement draws closer, to pay what are called 'additional voluntary contributions' – AVCs. You get tax relief, within certain limits, on the money you pay in, and you get a bigger pension in return.

Until recently employees were tied to the AVC scheme offered by their employer. If the employer chose not to offer one at all, that was tough luck. Now, though, anything goes and you can pick any AVC plan you like, and there are a growing number available, particularly from building societies and life companies.

A 1988 reform will also make it possible for employees to opt out of their employer's pension fund itself – as long as a substitute plan is taken out elsewhere. It seems clear most employees will stay where they are, out of confusion and inertia if nothing else – and there is something to be said for staying put, unless, perhaps, you are the sort of person likely to switch jobs a large number of times during your life, or even go it alone and set up your own business.

By the time you have passed through the basic stages of being educated, opening your first building society and bank accounts, finding a job, investing in unit trusts, buying a home, getting married, joining a pension fund and taking out life cover, you may not feel inclined to look any further so far as financial planning is concerned. That would be a mistake!

There is never an ideal time of life to set aside risk capital. There is always something more sensible to spend the money on! But by the time you are in your thirties and forties your life should be sufficiently ordered for you to take some risk. Buying stocks and shares, either directly or through a unit or investment trust, is one way of aiming for real growth. A more risky avenue is to put money into a Business Expansion Scheme. The tax reliefs available when you invest and when you reap your profit make the risk of putting money into often untested small businesses a worthwhile one.

And PEPs – Personal Equity Plans – will, one hopes, be given a radical face-lift by the Government to make them worthwhile too. At present these are a classic example of a good idea badly executed. You pay no tax on dividend income, but the value of exemption is swallowed up in management fees, and you pay no tax on capital gains – but as the maximum investment is £3,000 a year, gains are very unlikely to be big enough to take you into the gains tax net anyway.

Retirement is something approached with mixed feelings by most people. We pretend to be looking forward to a rest after a lifetime of work, but we wonder how to afford it.

Apart from the various pensions we may have earned, pensioners are often living in what can become a new source of income – their home. Home income plans are not new, but they are increasingly popular. There are two basic types, one involving selling your home to a finance company and the other involving mortgaging your home. Both produce a lump sum which is then invested to generate an annuity payable for the rest of your life, and both sorts of scheme allow you to live in the property for the rest of your days. When you die, the company takes possession of the property and sells it.

The difference between the two schemes is that in the first the company actually owns your home and gets the benefit of any rise in value. In the second, you own the property and you get the benefit of any rise, which means you can have something to leave your heirs after the mortgage is paid off, or you can even go back to the annuity company and take out a second home income plan based on the new, higher value of your home.

Shakespeare's ages of man come to an end with second childhood ('sans teeth, sans eyes, sans taste, sans everything') and oblivion. But financial planning includes making out a will and keeping it up to date at all stages of your life, reflecting the different needs of your beneficiaries and your different wishes so far as fulfilling those needs is concerned.

Inheritance Tax, like its predecessors, estate duty and death duties, is largely a voluntary tax. By giving assets away, making maximum use of annual exemptions, setting up trust funds, and making sure you do not die with a large amount of personal wealth, you can minimise or eliminate the tax man's share of your wordly goods; a fine aim with which to take your leave.

Tony Hetherington

2 Nest Eggs and Cash Flow

Good money management not only makes sense – it can also make money. It's not how much money you have, but what you do with it that counts. As Sam Weller observed in *Pickwick Papers*, 'It's a wery remarkable circumstance, sir, that poverty and oysters always seem to go together'. If like me you have a taste for oysters…keep reading. This chapter is dedicated to us. But it is not a Dickensian dialectic on the virtues of thrift. When you've finished reading you will still be treating yourself to liberal helpings of the good things in life. And enjoying them all the more in the knowledge that your money is making money, while you rest and play.

Each March the Chancellor of the Exchequer emerges from No 11 Downing Street with his little red box and begins the annual round of begging Peter to pay Paul. A penny on here and a half-penny off there, on and on he drones. Gladstone holds the record for the longest Budget speech. In 1853 he pontificated for four hours and forty-five minutes. Boring the ritual may be, but without an annual budget the country would come to a standstill. The Chancellor is balancing the books and deciding how much we can afford to spend and on what. He builds in contingency funds in case his forecasts are awry. He is shaping our lives for the coming twelve months and he has some of the best brains in Britain to help him to do it.

Drawing up a family budget is a microcosm of that exercise – but it will likely prove as contentious and unpopular as the Government's efforts. (Speeches are usually best avoided.) But planning a budget is crucial. It is the starting point of all sound financial management. 'No good at sums' is not a valid excuse. Buy a pocket calculator – or better still, learn to add up.

There is no mystique or magic to devising a budget. All you need to do is draw up a long list of all household expenses throughout the year, add them up, add say five per cent for inflation, and divide the answer by twelve. Be as precise as possible in your estimations. If your gas bill is £116.98, do not jot down £100. With inflation you could be out by £20. Such a margin of error on each figure soon undermines the exercise.

If at this stage your annual outgoings grossly exceed your income, forget what I said about Dickensian dialectics and invest in a copy of *David Copperfield*. Read and digest the unhappy tale of Mr Micawber, and then carefully consider where you can cut back, even if it means moving to a smaller house. Your creditors will force you to economise in the end, so the sooner you do it for yourself the better.

Keep and file old bills and receipts, as they help with forward projections, are proof of purchase in the event of a complaint, fire or burglary, and add a little light relief to future budget-making meetings. Have you noticed how rarely bills fall?

To button down every penny, it can help to keep a pocket book with you for a few weeks and make a note of everything you spend, to make sure you are accurately accounting for all expenditure. I tried this once and discovered I spent three times as much as I thought on 'miscellaneous'. Little wonder the budget never balanced.

Dividing by twelve tells you in theory how much you need to earn each month to make it through the year in the black, but of course bills are like buses, they always come in twos or threes. Make a monthly chart showing when each bill is due. If two or three stinkers generally arrive together, try and reschedule them. Most large bills, such as rates, gas, electricity and telephone, can be paid by monthly instalments. This can simplify cash flow, but it will mean paying for a good part of the bill a couple of months before you need to. Pay all your bills by monthly budget and you are parting with a sizeable sum which could be earning you interest elsewhere. It could make all the difference between oysters and offals.

Managing Your Cash Flow

Having taken the big political decisions on spending over the next twelve months, you must now throw the dice to begin your journey across the snakes and ladders board of practical management. At certain times of the year you will be climbing

Budget Forecast

You can design your own budget forecast, but here is an example.

	JAN	FEB	MAR	APR	MAY	JUN	JUL	AUG	SEP	OCT	NOV	DEC	TOTAL
mortgage/rent	350	350	350	350	350	350	350	350	350	350	350	350	£4200
rates				300						300			£600
water rates				85						85			£170
gas			200			100			80			200	£580
electricity		50			50			50			50		£200
telephone		80			80			80			80		£320
insurances:													
contents	95												£95
buildings			130										£130
life	30	30	30	30	30	30	30	30	30	30	30	30	£360
health	10	10	10	10	10	10	10	10	10	10	10	10	£120
car								250					£250
car tax								100					£100
petrol	20	20	20	20	20	20	20	20	20	20	20	20	£240
servicing	75						75						£150
childcare/school fees	200	200	200	200	200	200	200	200	200	200	200	200	£2400
loan/repayment	50	50	50	50	50	50	50	50	50	50	50	50	£600
misc	20	20	20	20	20	20	20	20	20	20	20	20	£240
TOTALS	850	810	1010	1065	810	780	755	1160	760	1065	810	880	TOTAL £10755
													£11292 plus5%inflation

monthly contributions £941 × 12 = £11292

the ladder to success with money in the bank. At other times you will be on the slippery slide to ruin, unable to meet your commitments. So where should you keep money not needed in the short term, and where should you borrow from when your money just won't stretch?

Surprisingly some 20 per cent of the population deals exclusively in cash, and less than 50 per cent has a credit card. But unless you receive a weekly pay packet you will need some kind of current account into which your salary can be paid.

There are two golden rules here. Firstly, never pay bank charges unless borrowing money. Remember Lewis Carroll's little ditty dedicated to bank clerks: 'He thought he saw a banker's clerk descending from the bus, he looked again and saw it was a hippopotamus. If this should stay and dine, he said, there won't be much for us'.

And secondly, earn interest wherever possible. Money makes money; make sure yours is working for you.

A **current account** is traditionally held with one of the major clearing banks. You will receive a cheque book and guarantee card, cash card for access to funds when the bank is closed, regular statements and facilities for paying cheques through a standing order or direct debit. With a standing order, sometimes called a bankers' order, you instruct the bank to pay a bill. With a direct debit, the organisation receiving the money presents the bill. In the future, Eftpos may replace the cheque book. This is the electronic transfer of funds at point of sale, and means your bank account will be automatically debited when you purchase your goods.

Current Account PLUS: They are simple to use and do not normally incur charges while the account remains in credit. **MINUS**: They do not pay interest on positive balances and you only need to slip out of credit for one day with most accounts, to receive a hefty bill for charges for a whole quarter.

Some current accounts like the Midland's **Vector** are free from bank charges even when the account is in the red, and also offer a small interest-free overdraft facility. You pay a quarterly service fee to the bank instead. These are designed for busy high-earners, who do not always know whether they are in credit.

Vector PLUS: If you are already regularly paying charges, it banishes worries over whether your account is in credit or not, and the size of any pending bank charges. **MINUS**: If you do not pay charges you will be paying for services you can already enjoy for free.

Bank Budget Accounts can take the strain out of averaging out the bills while you even out the monthly allowance. You pay in your minimum monthly contribution and the bank pays the bills as they arise, regardless of whether there are sufficient funds in the account to meet them. But you are charged interest whenever the account is overdrawn. If you have serious cash flow problems and would be forced to borrow elsewhere anyway, budget accounts have a use.

Budget Account PLUS: Takes the worry about the bills off your shoulders and the interest rate charged is usually in line with bank personal loan charges. **MINUS**: The account earns you no interest when in credit, and may incur banking charges.

Revolving Credit Accounts are a variation on this theme, although they are designed for funding large purchases such as a sailboard or CD player, rather than running the household budget. You pay a fixed amount of up to £100 into the account each month and you can then borrow up to thirty times that sum immediately. While the account is in credit you receive interest; you pay interest to the bank when you are in the red. For a larger revolving credit of up to £15,000, homeowners reserve accounts provide access to loans secured on your house. Needless to say, the amount of interest the bank pays you when you are in the black is a great deal less than the amount you have to pay it when you are not.

Revolving Credit Account PLUS: Allows greater shopping flexibility. **MINUS**: You would get a better rate of interest on credit balances elsewhere. The interest rate on negative balances can sometimes be above that charged for personal loans.

High Interest Cheque Accounts are also available from some banks. These offer limited banking facilities, while earning a competitive interest rate. You can only use cheques to draw fairly substantial amounts of cash or to pay large bills.

High Interest Cheque Account PLUS: Your money is earning interest, while you have immediate access. **MINUS**: Not very flexible. Initial deposits are high at more than £2,000 and minimum withdrawals and cheques can be as high as £250.

Many building societies offer personal cheque accounts

with a range of banking services, while paying interest. Some of these accounts offer all the services available with a clearing bank current account, such as standing orders, direct debits, cheque guarantee card, personal loans and overdrafts. The interest earned on these accounts will be more than you would realise in a bank's current account, budget account or revolving credit account.

Building Society Cheque Account PLUS: (and it's a big plus): Your money is earning you an attractive rate of interest all the time it is in the account. **MINUS**: Not all accounts offer a comprehensive range of banking services. Check services before buying. But even those with more limited banking facilities can be a useful alternative to a bank account, if used in conjunction with a credit card.

Finance Houses and other Financial Institutions such as Save & Prosper, M&G, HFC Bank, Oppenheimer Money Management or Phillips & Drew also offer **high interest cheque accounts**. These accounts follow the pattern of the banks' version, with high initial deposits and limited withdrawal facilities. **PLUS**: You earn interest. **MINUS**: Some accounts levy charges, which can wipe out any gains made on interest. They do not normally provide a cheque guarantee card, which limits their usefulness. Unless you have a branch of the finance house in your town, access to cash will be more onerous than at a local bank branch.

A National Girobank Account operates in a similar fashion to a clearing bank account but post offices form the branch network. Overdraft interest rates tend to be steep, but bank charges are only levied for the days overdrawn – not the whole quarter. **PLUS**: Convenient if you regularly visit the post office. **MINUS**: You cannot cash cheques in all banks.

A National Savings Ordinary Account also uses the post office counter as its point of sale. It pays a reasonable interest and offers limited banking facilities. (See page 34.)

Where to Borrow Money

Would you credit it, but having drawn up an impeccable budget and picked the best of the bunch from the cash flow account list, you still can't find enough spare cash for a trip to the oyster shop? Don't worry, the Chancellor usually has the same problem – so he borrows billions.

You won't need quite so much (we hope); but as long as you are in control of your financial affairs, there is nothing whatsoever wrong with taking out a loan to indulge your fancy, be it oysters or onyx. As a general guideline, loan repayments should not exceed a fifth of surplus income after budget deductions. So which loans are economic in the long run, and how do you qualify for one?

Once you buy a house, open a bank account, buy shares and acquire credit cards, your name begins to appear on various credit-rating agency lists which are used to assess your credit-worthiness. Get a bad record on one of these lists and you may find great difficulty in obtaining credit for years to come.

Credit scoring is like playing Trivial Pursuits without drinking – not very amusing. You answer obscure questions about your personal life and then if your score is high enough, you get to pick a card. A points system is supposed to rule out subjective human judgement. You will gain different points depending on whether you own your own home, what the post code is, whether you have a credit card, how long you have worked for your employer, and so on.

Interest-free Loans are the best way to borrow, if you can get them. Many department stores have a regular interest-free loan facility at set times each year, so it can be worth waiting to buy large items. But do not be too enthusiastic about three-month interest-free credit offers – you almost get that with your credit card.

Interest-free Loans PLUS: It costs you nothing. **MINUS**: Some shops inflate prices, so you are effectively paying interest in the purchase price.

Outside the large chains it can be worth offering to pay with three or four post-dated cheques. If you are bold enough to ask, it is surprising how many retailers will agree, or offer a compromise. Catalogue shopping has its own built-in credit system, but in most cases the prices are heavily inflated to account for the credit.

If you cannot find an interest-free loan, the banks or building societies are the best alternatives. If you are borrowing for home improvements always increase your mortgage rather than ask for a personal loan. The interest rate will be lower, but it will no longer qualify for mortgage interest tax relief.

When arranging any kind of loan, the key phrase to watch

is the APR – annual percentage rate. This takes into account not only what you pay in interest, but any service charge or arrangement fee. The lower the APR the cheaper the loan, and you can be confident there will be no hidden costs.

A Bank or Building Society Overdraft is designed for coping with short-term cash problems. The rate of interest charged will be a percentage above base rates, depending on how valued a customer you are.

Overdraft PLUS: If you are a valued customer, interest rates will be low. **MINUS**: Banks and building societies are reluctant to grant them except as a short-term expediency. There may be an arrangement fee, and your account will be subject to bank charges once it is in the red.

A Personal Loan from a Bank or Building Society is the best option if you are trying to finance a major purchase like a car, holiday or home furnishings. You can normally borrow up to £5,000 for a period of one to five years.

Personal Loan PLUS: Interest rates will be competitive and there will be no hidden charges. **MINUS**: Banks and building societies are cautious lenders, and may turn you down unless you are already a good customer, having proved your credit worthiness. They may not be flexible about early repayment once the loan is structured. An overdraft could be cheaper, if you can persuade the bank manager. You need to do the sums carefully.

A loan secured against your home or portfolio of shares is available from banks and building societies for larger sums, which can be repaid over longer periods or over the life of the home loan.

Secured Loan PLUS: The APR could be as much as five per cent cheaper than an unsecured loan, and it may be the only method available for borrowing large sums. **MINUS**: If you default you may lose your home.

Credit Cards are an excellent short-term borrowing device because by timing your purchase correctly, you can enjoy up to seven weeks' interest-free credit. Visa and Access are the two most common credit cards.

On qualifying for a card you will be given a credit limit, which sets the ceiling for each month's spend. If the limit seems a bit low, ask for it to be increased. If the account has been responsibly handled, the request is normally greeted sympathetically. You must pay a minimum of five per cent of your outstanding balance within twenty-one days of receiving a monthly statement. After that you pay interest on outstanding balances. It is always best to clear the balances.

Credit Card PLUS: If you settle the bill each month you can get around seven weeks' free credit, depending on the date of purchase. There are no charges and you get a detailed print out with each month's statement of what you have spent where. So if you are broke in January when the sales are on, you can cut the cost of your clothing bill by using your credit card to pick up bargains. Credit cards offer flexible credit – *you* decide how much to repay each month after the statutory minimum.

They also provide a number of perks. If you pay for something costing more than £100 by credit card, and you fail to receive the goods, or are dissatisfied with them, you can sue the credit card company if the firm involved fails to compensate you; perhaps because it has gone bust. This is particularly useful when booking a holiday. Buy travel with your card and free life insurance of £50,000 is included while you are in transit.

Credit Card MINUS: Interest over a long period is expensive when compared with a personal loan. It can tempt you to buy things you can't afford. If that's the case, tear it up. The bank will insist you do in time anyway.

A loan against an existing life insurance policy or personal pension plan which has been running for a number of years can sometimes be arranged.

Insurance or Pension Loan PLUS: You are effectively borrowing from yourself and the loan in some cases may not need to be repaid until the policy matures. **MINUS**: You need to own a policy which has built up a sizeable value and you will have to pay a commercial rate of interest. Also you are undermining the value of a policy which could be crucial to the financial well-being of your family if you died suddenly, or to you when you retire.

Cheap Loans are sometimes available through credit unions. These are groups of people who club together to offer loans to those in need at a low interest rate. The Citizens Advice Bureau should be able to tell you if there is one operating in your area. **PLUS**: Interest rates should be competitive. **MINUS**: They are few and far between.

Most large department stores will offer credit accounts

or charge cards, which are another convenient shopping aid provided the bill is paid each month. However APRs will vary considerably from store to store and should be studied carefully before you commit yourself. **PLUS**: Convenient, and allow credit interest-free for a short period. **MINUS**: Some interest charges are exorbitant. They are almost always higher than the interest on credit cards.

With **hire purchase** you sign a legal agreement allowing you to hire the goods with the intention of ultimately owning them. The final instalment makes them yours. **PLUS**: It may be your only method of borrowing if your credit scoring is low. **MINUS**: It can be very expensive.

Finance houses will give loans directly, and sometimes operate mail marketing campaigns. **PLUS**: Lending criteria may be less cautious than the banks and building societies. **MINUS**: They cover their risk by charging higher interest rates.

If you do find yourself slipping further and further into debt, perhaps because you have lost your job, or your marriage is breaking up, seek advice before the tangled web of debts gets completely out of control.

Make a clear list of all your debts, and the periods over which they are owed, and your income. If with a few months of stringent economy you still cannot meet the debts, speak to your bank, building society or Citizens Advice Bureau. They will help you sort out which debts can and must be paid, and what you are going to do with the others. Loans can often be extended.

Where to Invest Your Contingency Fund?

You will not find yourself in the position outlined above if you build a contingency fund into your day-to-day money management regime. The Chancellor sets aside some £5 billion or so a year for unforeseen emergencies. As Mr Micawber knew to his cost, 'Accidents will occur in the best regulated families.' A rainy-day fund would have saved him many a headache (not to mention prison sentence). How much you need to set aside for unexpected bills or family disasters will depend on the size of your overheads, but £500 or £1,000 in an immediate access risk-free account should help you to sleep more soundly at night. But where should you invest your contingency fund so that it is earning the maximum interest, but where at the same time you can get your hands on it as soon as the wind gets up?

You will not go far wrong with an interest-bearing account with a bank, building society or National Savings, depending on current interest rates, how long you are required to tie your money up and your current tax position.

If you already have accessible funds in such an account and require further rearguard risk-free financial defence, you could consider local authority bonds, government stocks, money market funds, or off-shore currency funds. Your present and future tax positions are major considerations when deciding where to place your money on deposit. Thousands of non-taxpaying investors pay tax needlessly each year.

Banks, building societies and local authorities pay interest net of composite rate tax. This is the tax deducted from investment earnings, normally fractionally lower than standard rate tax. If you are a standard rate taxpayer no further tax is due. Higher rate taxpayers must declare the earnings on their tax return and are further liable at their highest rate. For this purpose, incidentally, the interest is 'grossed up' using the *full* basic tax rate, not the lower composite rate. Non-taxpayers will not be able to reclaim tax, so children and pensioners should consider investing elsewhere. A non-working wife's investment earnings are currently deemed her husband's income for tax purposes, although this will change after 1990. Composite rate tax is fractionally lower than standard rate because it is administratively easier for the Inland Revenue to collect, so collecting costs are correspondingly lower. The reduced margin also acknowledges that tax is being over-paid by those who, strictly speaking, are not liable.

Why did the nest egg cross the road? To make sure he was getting the best return he could. Before investing, compare interest rates between the various institutions. Either contact a handful of your local banks and building societies, or compare tables in personal finance magazines. Teletext television also has a regularly updated interest rates' guide.

Unless you invest in a fixed interest account interest rates will be variable, that is they will go up and down in line with market forces. You may find little to choose between the rates offered by the big building societies or the banks, and probably pick a local branch for convenience. Some of the small societies, hungry for business, pay interest rates above those offered by the large groups. These accounts are to be recommended, particularly if one has a branch nearby.

There are three key phrases when comparing interest rates – 'net', 'gross' and 'compounded annual rate'. Banks and building societies quote their interest rates 'net'. That is less composite rate tax. This tells you the final net yield for a standard rate taxpayer. When interest rates are quoted 'gross', tax has not yet been deducted. If you do not pay tax, this is the sum you keep. All taxpayers will be liable to further deductions at their highest rate.

A final and crucial phrase is 'compounded annual rate'. Interest rates are further complicated because some institutions pay interest annually, some twice a year, and some even once a month.

If you are paid interest monthly and those earnings are rolled up into the investment, at the end of the year you will have earned more than with an account paying the same interest but only once a year. The compounded annual rate tells you how much interest you will earn throughout the year, taking into account the roll-up factor.

Both Banks and Building Societies Offer **Basic Deposit Accounts**. You deposit your money with the institution, normally in return for a passbook, and you collect the cash, plus some interest at a later date.

Deposit Account PLUS: Your money is safe. In theory you are safer with a deposit account than with the higher earning building society share account, because should a building society run into financial problems a depositor has first call on any available funds. However, as the building society compensation scheme refunds 90 per cent up to £20,000, the extra protection offered by the deposit account is negligible. **MINUS**: The interest is the lowest around, and may not even equal inflation. They have little to recommend them.

Building Society Ordinary Share Accounts pay a marginally higher rate of interest than the deposit accounts. With a building society share account you become a member of the society, and can share in the benefits that membership will bring, such as preferential access to home loans.

Share Account PLUS: Initial deposits are as low as £1. **MINUS**: More attractive interest rates can be found elsewhere for larger sums.

Bank and Building Society High Interest or 'Gold'

Accounts pay a tiered rate of interest on larger lump sums. Earnings go up in bands, so you will earn half a per cent extra interest depending on whether you have, say, £1,000, £5,000 or £10,000 invested. Such accounts have much to recommend them as a safe haven for contingency funds. Building societies traditionally offered the best rate of return, but fierce competition has seen the banks periodically leading on interest rates. It is a matter of checking as you deposit.

Gold Account PLUS: An attractive rate of interest, while maintaining immediate access. **MINUS**: High minimum deposits of normally £500 or £1,000. Composite rate tax cannot be reclaimed by non-taxpayers.

Term and Notice Accounts have been largely replaced by the 'gold' accounts, although a number of institutions are still offering them. Both these accounts restrict accessibility. With a term share, you pledge money for a period of perhaps a year or several years. With notice accounts, you are required to give notice of intention to withdraw – normally 90 days. Immediate access is sometimes available, but only at the cost of loss of interest.

Term and Notice Accounts PLUS: You will receive an attractive rate of interest, sometimes slightly more than is on offer with a 'gold' account. **MINUS**: Minimum investments start at £500. You are surrendering immediate access to your funds. Early redemption means loss of interest.

Building societies and banks have designed accounts specifically for children, which offer free gifts ranging from cameras, files and pens to T-shirts and bags. They often run clubs with regular comics and competitions. Although children are strictly speaking better off with an account which pays interest gross, such as National Savings, many youngsters like the extras on offer with net paying accounts. These accounts also offer instant access, while a National Savings investment account requires a month's notice of withdrawal.

In any case, if children's savings were originally gifts from their parents, any interest arising is strictly speaking counted as the parent's own, for tax purposes – and taxed at the parent's marginal rate. Investments paying gross interest should be kept as a home for gifts from elsewhere – from grandparents, uncles and aunts.

Many building societies and banks run monthly income accounts paying interest more frequently than other accounts, which can be useful for pensioners or others without a regular income. They also offer regular savings accounts which pay a higher interest than an ordinary share account. Normally only one withdrawal is permitted each year on such accounts, and you are allowed to miss one contribution. It is advisable to move lumps built up in savings accounts to higher yield accounts as soon as possible.

Savings Accounts, High Interest Deposit Accounts and Term Accounts are also available from some of the same financial institutions offering high interest cheque accounts. They offer what are called money market rates of interest: the rates which are charged to corporations for short-term borrowing. **PLUS**: Interest rates will be competitive. **MINUS**: Access to funds will not be as easy as with a local bank or building society. Interest rates may not be as high as banks' high interest or building society 'gold' accounts.

If you are a non-taxpayer, such as a child or pensioner, or a higher rate taxpayer, the National Savings range of products should not be ignored. All accounts pay interest gross while Savings Certificates are free from tax completely, which can be attractive to higher rate taxpayers. Interest rates are variable on some of these accounts and standard rate taxpayers may find more competitive deals elsewhere.

National Savings Investments were introduced during the First World War to raise money for the war effort, and are used today to help fund the public sector borrowing requirement. When the PSBR falls there is less pressure on the Treasury to raise funds, and interest rates can suffer accordingly. No one likes to pay interest on money they do not need to borrow. So despite the tax concessions it can sometimes be a close run decision on whether to go into National Savings or a building society.

The NS range of investment bonds includes a deposit bond and an income bond, which have differing minimum investment requirements, notice of withdrawals and interest rates. You can invest in a deposit bond with £50, but need £1,000 to buy an income bond.

Investment Bonds PLUS: Interest is paid gross. **MINUS**: Six weeks' notice is needed for withdrawals for the income and deposit bond. Taxpayers may be able to find as competitive rates of interest elsewhere without tying their money up.

An NS Investment Account has a low minimum investment and is probably the best account available for children. **PLUS**: Minimum investment £5 and interest is paid gross. One of the best rates of interest available for small investments. **MINUS**: A month's notice is necessary for withdrawals.

The NS Ordinary Account also has a low minimum investment and offers some money management facilities. Another attraction is that the first £70 of interest each year is tax free. **PLUS**: You can use it to pay any bills which can normally be paid through a post office, and withdraw cash daily. This could be useful if you regularly visit a post office rather than a bank. Tax-free earnings could be attractive to higher rate taxpayers. **MINUS**: Interest rate is poor if you are not liable to tax.

National Savings Certificates pay interest at a fixed rate for a five-year term which is free from all tax – a big bonus for higher rate taxpayers. You can also buy index-linked certificates. **PLUS**: Tax-free earnings. Minimum investment £25. **MINUS**: Maximum investment £1,000 (in the current issue, the 33rd) although you can reinvest up to £5,000 from the proceeds of previous matured certificate issues. To qualify for attractive returns the certificates must be held for normally five years – so you have to be prepared to lock your money away. Once the five-year term is up, the more recent issues of Certificates are automatically transferred on to the Common Extension Rate (CER). The interest continues to be tax-free, but the CER is variable, not fixed.

NS Yearly Plans allow regular contributions for twelve months into a savings plan earning a fixed rate of interest. **PLUS**: If interest rates are falling, the fixed earnings become attractive. **MINUS**: If the plan is cashed in before the year is up, you earn no interest at all.

Local Authority Bonds are loans to a local authority in the same way that National Savings are loans to the Government. You have to invest for a set period, and interest rates are fixed from the outset. They can be bought by writing direct to local authorities. A regularly updated list of bonds is available from Cipfa Sterling, 65 London Wall, London EC2M 5TU.

Local Authority Bonds PLUS: The rate of interest is fixed when you buy the bond, so if interest rates are falling, you are locked into high earnings. **MINUS**: Interest is paid net of basic rate tax, which cannot be reclaimed by non-taxpayers.

If you change your mind you cannot get your money back. There is no early redemption, unless you die, which is rather an extreme step to take. If interest rates are rising, your money might do better elsewhere.

Local Authority 'Yearling' Bonds are more flexible because they can be traded on the stock market like shares. Interest rates are fixed as the name suggests for twelve months. But trading could involve a capital gain or loss. **PLUS**: Greater flexibility. **MINUS**: Involves a risk, as capital value could depreciate if interest movements are against you.

Offshore Money Market Funds allow you to enjoy money market interest rates either by placing your money on deposit with a financial institution, or investing in a currency fund. These funds are run outside mainland Britain in places like Guernsey and the Cayman Islands. You buy shares in the fund rather as you do in a unit trust. The profits of the fund are used to pay interest on your investment which you receive gross. Such funds are not permitted to operate onshore at present, but changes to the rules governing unit trusts envisage that money market funds could be operating onshore within a few years.

If you invest in a sterling fund you earn interest at a rate normally set daily, but which will be generally in line with that offered by top-rate building society accounts. If you decide to invest in another currency, the value of your investment will go up and down against the pound, so you are taking a risk. You may want to invest in DMs, for example, because you have just sold German equities and want to maintain your DM exposure until you go back into equities there. Or you may be planning overseas travel, and want to underpin the cost of your holiday by buying into the currency of your destination which is climbing against sterling.

It is important to remember that once you invest offshore the investor protection measures of British Law are invalid. Many of the companies operating offshore are the same as the institutions selling investments in London. But even big financial institutions can get their sums wrong in times of crisis. When investing overseas, only invest with companies with impeccable reputations to maintain on the mainland.

If you want to gamble on the Currency Markets you could buy into a managed currency fund rather than back your hunches on a single foreign currency. Currencies are volatile

and movements frequently rapid and unexpected. By spread-
ing your investment in a portfolio of currencies managed by
a professional fund manager, you should reduce the likelihood
of badly burning your fingers.

There are two kinds of funds: a distributor fund which
distributes income, or an accumulator fund where income is
rolled up. Interest on the distributor fund is subject to income
tax, and any capital gain on the currency fluctuations is liable
for capital gains tax.

Accumulator funds defer paying tax until the gain is
realised, then income tax must be paid on both income and
capital growth. This has the advantage that if your tax position is likely to change, because you are about to retire, say,
or live abroad for a while, you can delay paying tax until
your tax rate is lower.

You can switch in and out of currencies easily and normally without charge, and no charge is made for currency
exchanges. There is an annual management charge of 0.75
per cent to 1.25 per cent, but interest rates should be quoted
net of this charge.

Currency Funds PLUS: Sterling currency funds will pay
a competitive interest gross and are risk-free. Offers almost
immediate access, although it may take a day or two to receive
your funds. **MINUS**: Foreign currency or managed funds are
volatile and probably too risky for your safe emergency kitty.
A three per cent initial charge is levied on managed funds.
Do remember, though, that if you live in this country you
are liable to income tax on *all* the income you receive, no
matter where it arises. Don't go offshore simply because you
want to escape the clutches of the Revenue; you can only do
that by cheating.

Gilts. *Liberté, Egalité, Fraternité.* Noble sentiments – but
as any civil servant will tell you, there is no such thing
as a free country. Running a country costs money, and
so the Treasury periodically borrows to meet its commitments. Its borrowings are called Government Securities, or
'gilts' for short.

If you buy the stocks when they are first issued, the
Government undertakes to pay you a fixed rate of interest
until their redemption date, when the loan is repaid at the
nominal price. If they are held until maturity, gilts are a
completely safe investment. You know exactly what you will

receive on redemption and how much you will earn each year until that date.

However, gilts can be traded on the stock market. If you buy a high interest stock at a time when interest rates begin to fall, you will be the envy of many and the capital value of your stock will rise accordingly. And as the capital value increases, so the yield decreases proportionately.

Gilts can be bought through a stockbroker or through the National Savings Stock Register at the post office. They are listed daily in quality newspapers and have rather strange sounding names like Treasury 1995. This tells you that the gilt matures in 1995. Listed also is the highest and lowest price for the gilt over the past year, what it stood at yesterday and the price change with the previous day in fractions of a pound. Finally it will tell you its yield.

Gilts are exempt from capital gains tax, which can be useful if you are nearing the threshold. Interest is payable and a stockbroker will normally deduct standard rate tax at source. Non-taxpayers can reclaim payments, and higher rate taxpayers will have to make up the balance on their tax returns. If you buy through the post office and the National Savings Stock Register interest is paid gross, which is useful for non-taxpayers – but it can be more expensive to deal in this way for larger sums.

Gilts PLUS: They can be flexible if you are prepared to risk trading. **MINUS**: For a safe investment your nest-egg may need to be tied up for several years. Buying them with a view to trading has all the risks associated with the stock market, and is not the place for funds which may be needed at a moment's notice.

Teresa Hunter

Information and Contacts
Building Societies Association
3 Savile Row
London W1X 1AF
01-437 0655

National Savings
Charles House
375 Kensington High Street
London W14 8SD

General telephone enquiries: 01–603 2000
(ext. 103/104) Mon–Fri 9am–4pm
Also enquire at Post Office

for local authority bond list:
CIPFA Sterling
65 London Wall
London EC2M 5TU
01–407 2767

3 Your Home

The editor of one of our national newspapers, not so many years ago, was reportedly horrified and incredulous when he found out one day by chance that most of his staff were large scale debtors, facing almost a lifetime of repaying their debts. The fact that these debts were called 'mortgages' did not lessen the horror for him. I suspect that for most of us, the idea of buying our homes with cash is equally absurd. Homes mean mortgages even more than Beanz meanz Heinz.

But while a few years ago, the mortgage shelves were half empty for much of the time, and there were precious few brands to choose from, today, in the late 1980s, the mortgage business has finally caught up with the rest of our consumer society. There's plenty of choice – and plenty of pitfalls for the unwary consumer.

The one thing you must not feel as you set off in search of a mortgage is grateful. The mortgage market is very competitive these days, with banks, building societies and some specialist mortgage lenders all fighting for their share. They need you at least as much as you need them, and the days of 'mortgage queues' have gone – if not for ever, at least for the foreseeable future.

For most people, these days, there is no sensible alternative

Table 1
Average House Prices

	£
1977	13,712
1978	15,674
1979	20,143
1980	23,514
1981	24,503
1982	24,577
1983	27,192
1984	29,648
1985	31,876
1986	38,000
1987	44,220

Source: *Building Societies Association and Department of the Environment*

to buying their own home. The privately rented sector has
been dying for years, and the public sector is also diminishing
as council tenants take up their rights to buy their own homes.
And who seriously would choose to live in those tower blocks?

Buying their own home has also been a financially rewarding experience for the vast majority of owner
occupiers today. As Table 1 shows, house prices have
climbed onwards and upwards for years. While the speed
of the increase has varied - especially when you take inflation into account - it's about as certain as anything is in
this world that you won't lose money by buying your
own property.

A couple of tax concessions also help to make the
exercise of home buying financially pleasant. In the first
place, interest payable on loans used for the purpose of
buying your principal residence attracts tax relief, at your
highest marginal rate. The fly in the ointment here is that
the relief is limited to the first £30,000 of the loan: an
ample figure when the limit was first introduced, but now
looking very mean indeed. There seems very little likelihood
that this will ever be increased; indeed, from time to time
there is great speculation that it might be abolished altogether, or that relief at higher rates might be withdrawn.

This relief is, in any case, limited to your 'principal private
residence' and cannot be used, for example, to buy a holiday
cottage. In addition, from August 1988, mortgage interest
relief is limited to one lot of £30,000 per property. Prior
to that, two (or more) unmarried people buying a property
between them could benefit from relief on £30,000 each; that
is now out of court.

The only exception to the former rule is if the nature
of your job requires you to live elsewhere - as a caretaker,
for example - but you want to buy your own property, for
retirement. This you can do, with the benefit of tax relief,
even though it is not strictly speaking your principal residence
while you are buying it.

The other major concession concerns capital gains tax:
there is none on the profits you realise when you sell your
main home. Once again, this concession does not apply to
gains made on second homes.

Mortgage Interest Relief at Source

This system (known as MIRAS for short) is now almost universally used. Borrowers make their interest payments net of basic rate tax relief. Higher rate taxpayers must still face the rigmarole of telling their tax inspector of the amount of interest they have paid – their lender should supply them with a MIRAS 5 form with all the appropriate details – and they will then pick up the tax relief by means of an increased tax coding.

The MIRAS system, incidentally, means that if the basic rate of tax is cut, then the net payments on a mortgage increase (less tax means less tax relief). The difference is not that great: at current mortgage rates, a penny off income tax would mean a borrower with an endowment mortgage would see his monthly payments increase by about a pound for each £10,000 borrowed, up to the £30,000 limit. (The examples given in this chapter assume a 25 per cent basic rate of tax.)

Before you start paying your mortgage, of course, you have to find your home, choose your lender, decide what sort of mortgage you want – and pay up a fair-sized sum for legal fees, stamp duty and the like.

The major question that most first-time buyers will be asking, even before they start looking, is 'how much can I borrow?' Lenders look at two things before they decide: the size of your income, and the value of the property concerned. All follow basically similar rules:

Income

A maximum loan equal to two-and-a-half (sometimes three) times your income, plus (if a couple) once times the secondary income.

Thanks to the Sex Discrimination Act, the 'secondary' income is simply the smaller of the two, not automatically defined as the woman's. Some lenders operate special low-start schemes where the multiples can be stretched up to three-and-a-half or even more. Their ideal choice for a low-start borrower is someone who has a clear career pattern in front of them with the virtually guaranteed prospect of significant pay increases in the future. If you're under pressure from the multiple of income point of view, it would be wise to consult a mortgage broker. Special schemes like these come and go; some may charge a higher rate of interest overall or have other drawbacks.

An alternative criterion used by some lenders is to take the sum of both incomes and offer a loan equal to twice that. If a couple's earnings are roughly equal, this formula produces the bigger sum; if one partner is earning a great deal more than the other, the 'three plus one' formula is the one to go for.

Valuation of Property

Given that your house is acting as security for the loan, it is not surprising that the lender takes a close interest – and it is the official valuation of the property, not the price you have agreed to pay, which matters.

The usual rule is that the loan must be for not more than 80 per cent of the valuation of the property. It is possible to

Table 2
The cost of mortgages per £1,000 per month for a 25–year term net of 25% tax, for mortgages up to £30,000

Mortgage rate % p.a.	Constant net repayment £	Endowment (interest only)★ £
9.75	7.36	6.09
10.00	7.48	6.24
10.25	7.60	6.41
10.50	7.73	6.56
10.75	7.85	6.71
11.00	7.98	6.87
11.25	8.11	7.03
11.50	8.23	7.18
11.75	8.36	7.34
12.00	8.49	7.50
12.25	8.62	7.65
12.50	8.75	7.81
12.75	8.88	7.97
13.00	9.01	8.12
13.25	9.14	8.28
13.50	9.27	8.44
13.75	9.41	8.59
14.00	9.54	8.75
14.25	9.68	8.90
14.50	9.81	9.06
14.75	9.95	9.22
15.00	10.08	9.34

★The endowment premium has to be added to establish the total cost of the mortgage per month.
Source: *Nationwide Anglia Building Society*

borrow more, although it is rare these days to find anyone lending 100 per cent of valuation.

If you do borrow more, you have to pay an extra charge known as a Mortgage Indemnity Guarantee. This is effectively insurance for the lender and will pay up if you fail to make your proper payments. Premiums for the guarantee vary from about 2.8 to 5.0 per cent of the extra amount borrowed above the 80 per cent mark.

This sum can usually be added to the mortgage, as long as it does not take the whole loan over 100 per cent of valuation, in which case it must be paid up front. Since it is the lender who takes out the policy (you merely pay for it) you cannot 'shop around' for the cheapest deal. The figure can be considerable – say, £600 if you're looking to borrow 95 per cent for a house valued at £100,000 – so you should look closely at the rate the lender is charging you, and also the level at which the Indemnity Guarantee comes into operation. Many lenders use the 80 per cent level, others use 75 per cent or even less.

If the amount you want to borrow is far less than the property's valuation, you could be in a good bargaining position. Some lenders offer special deals for borrowers who have plenty of 'equity' to put into their purchase, and you could benefit from, say, a quarter per cent reduction in the usual mortgage interest rate. Consult a mortgage broker. These deals are most common where all the figures involved are fairly high – there may be a minimum loan of £30,000 or £40,000.

Having established what you can borrow, the next question must be – how much will it cost me? Table 2 shows the net monthly payments for each £1,000 borrowed at a range of interest rates. These figures are net of basic rate tax only,

Table 3
Monthly Payments on Larger Loans

Size of loan	Repayment mortgage	Endowment Mortgage (interest only)
£40,000	£309.93	£272.47
£50,000	£401.58	£357.89
£60,000	£494.28	£443.31
£80,000	£680.62	£614.14
£100,000	£867.38	£784.97

Assuming a 25-year mortgage and an interest rate of 10%
Source: *Nationwide Anglia Building Society*

Table 4
Land Registry Fees

Purchase Price £	Fee★ £
0–15,000	20
15,001–20,000	25
20,001–25,000	30
25,001–30,000	40
30,001–35,000	50
35,001–40,000	60
40,001–45,000	70
45,001–50,000	80
50,001–60,000	90
60,001–70,000	100
70,001–80,000	125
80,001–90,000	150
90,001–100,000	175
100,001–150,000	200
150,001–200,000	225
200,001–300,000	250

★Assuming the house is already listed on the Registry; the fee for initial registration is slightly lower

assuming a rate of 25 per cent. With the endowment or pension mortgage, remember, the figures show only half the story. In addition to the interest on the loan, borrowers have to pay a regular monthly premium on their life or pension policy.

The figures also assume that you are not borrowing more than £30,000. If you are, there is no extra tax relief. Table 3 gives some examples of the monthly cost for larger loans.

The Costs of Buying

Stamp duty, valuations and solicitors' fees can all add up to an unpleasantly large sum which can be particularly depressing for the first-time buyer who is valiantly trying to save enough for a deposit. Some of the expenses associated with moving are avoidable; most are not.

Stamp duty is payable at the rate of 1 per cent on all properties costing more than £30,000, and is payable on the whole figure, not the excess over the limit. Land registry charges will take another chunk - some examples are shown in Table 4. Solicitors' fees are in theory avoidable if you are prepared to do your own conveyancing (for suggested reading, see the end of the chapter) but you will in any case have to pay the lender's legal fees.

Another inescapable expense is the valuation of the property, carried out for the lender. Many house buyers cut corners by relying on that valuation and not bothering to commission a separate survey of their property. This is silly. Apart from anything else, if the survey is less than perfect you have an excellent excuse for going back to your vendor and trying to negotiate a lower price for the property.

The cost of the survey will vary considerably, depending on the nature of the property and also the firm concerned; it could be worth shopping around. You should make sure that the survey also includes a valuation for the lender, so you will escape the additional valuation charge.

Some lenders offer a half-way house between a simple valuation and a full structural survey: the Halifax Building Society, for example, offers a 'Homebuyer's Report and Valuation' which, while not as detailed as a full survey, should cover all the major points. Examples of the cost are shown in Table 5.

Solicitors' fees for conveyancing have come down considerably since competition, in the shape of licensed conveyancers, came on to the scene. It is definitely worth shopping around, but remember you'll need them to be efficient and cheapest is not necessarily best. Since you also pay for the legal work undertaken on behalf of the lender, you should make sure the firm you choose is also acceptable to the lender - otherwise

Table 5
Cost of Homebuyers Report and Valuation

Purchase price	
£	£
15,000	100
20,000	105
25,000	120
30,000	130
40,000	145
50,000	160
60,000	175
75,000	210
90,000	220
100,000	230
101,000 to 150,000	£10 extra per £10,000
Over 150,000	By arrangement

Source: *Halifax Building Society*

they can insist on using another company and the cost will almost certainly be higher.

If you are determined to do your own conveyancing, do read up on the subject first. It is generally thought sensible only to attempt it if you are buying a freehold property which is already entered on the land registry. If it is not, you will have to search back through fifteen years of records to establish title. Leasehold properties can also present problems and it would be wise to have a professional eye running through the terms of the lease.

If you are selling as well as buying you are likely to have estate agents' fees as well. If you can succeed in selling your house yourself, you will probably save a great deal of money, but there are costs involved such as advertising which you'll have to pay upfront. With estate agents, the usual rule is: no sale - no fee.

Estate agents, like solicitors, have started to compete in recent years and the consumers' rallying cry of 'shop around' applies equally here. Fees have tumbled recently and many agents charge 1 per cent of the sale price whereas a few years ago they were charging 2 per cent. It is not usually worth placing your house with more than one agent at a time as the fee increases for a joint or multiple agency.

On the question of whether to accept a 'For Sale' board disfiguring the front of your home (you can refuse) I can only say that I owe my last house sale to such a board, which caught the eye of a passer-by who promptly decided the house was for him.

Finally on the matter of costs, some lenders charge a special arrangement fee: either based on a percentage of the loan, or typically, a flat £100. Building societies in general do not make such a charge; some of the banks and specialist mortgage lenders do.

Mortgages
What's on offer and how should you choose?

If you think the answer to this question is simple - 'look at the quoted interest rate and choose the lowest' - then you might have to think again. In the first place, you have a choice as to how you are going to repay the loan - bit by bit over the years, or in one fell swoop at the end of the term with the proceeds from some savings scheme - and secondly there are choices connected with the interest rate: do you want a fixed or variable interest rate, one linked to LIBOR (London Inter Bank Offered Rate) or perhaps a 'cap and collar' arrangement appeals to you? Of these terms, more later. First there is the basic choice as to how you will repay the loan.

Repayment mortgages

The simplest option: each month you will back a small amount of the capital borrowed as well as interest on the loan still outstanding. Most repayment mortgages are set up to last for 25 years and the actual amount of capital you pay back in the early years is very small. At the end of year one, you will have paid off approximately £135 from a £10,000 loan, for example. The proportion of capital repayment within each monthly instalment rises over the years, so that by year 23 or 24 you are paying almost entirely capital not interest.

Repayment mortgages do not have to last for 25 years; you can choose a shorter or longer time span, though most lenders will insist the mortgage is paid off before your retirement. Not surprisingly, the shorter the time period, the more expensive it is.

Repayment mortgages have a couple of attractive points. If you move house after a few years, you may have paid off a tidy sum from the mortgage debt which will come in useful for the next purchase. They can also, in theory, offer some useful flexibility if you find difficulty in meeting the payments. Many lenders will allow their borrowers to extend the term of the mortgage to help them out of temporary problems. Extending the term means that the portion of capital paid back each month falls. In emergencies, borrowers can sometimes be allowed to go on an 'interest only' basis.

Not all lenders are so understanding; building societies tend to be kinder than some of their recently arrived competitors.

There are a few minus points to repayment mortgages, however. While not disadvantages in themselves, they compare unfavourably to the other major method of paying your mortgage, by using an endowment.

In the first place, there is no in-built protection if you die before the end of the mortgage term. If you have any dependants - or even if, though both of you are earning, you are financially interdependent - it is really vital to have some sort of life assurance policy that will pay off the outstanding mortgage sum if you die.

Many lenders actually insist on your taking out such a policy, though most of the building societies do not. The cost of a tailor-made Mortgage Protection Policy is not that great – particularly at younger ages – but you should add this to your monthly payments if you're doing a cost comparison between repayment and endowment mortgages. As an example, the monthly premium for a £25,000 mortgage over 25 years would be around £6 for a couple aged 30 and 28 respectively, and nearly £10 a month if they were ten years older at the outset. Like so much else, the cost can vary quite considerably depending on the life company chosen; an insurance broker could help here.

Secondly, when you finally reach the end of the mortgage term, you will no doubt have a warm glow of satisfaction, but that is all. There is no cash surplus for you to run riot with. If you like the idea of that, you may decide instead on an endowment mortgage.

Endowment Mortgages

With an endowment mortgage, you have a package of two separate elements. You pay interest only on the loan each month, and make a separate payment to a with-profits life assurance policy, set to run for the same number of years as the mortgage. On maturity, the proceeds of the policy should be more than enough to pay off the loan in its entirety – leaving you with a (tax-free) surplus to spend as you like.

Most of the premiums you pay go towards building up this sum, but you are also automatically covered if you die before the end of the term. Given that – whether you live or die – you are dependent on that policy to pay off your mortgage, lenders like to keep control of it, and will insist that it is 'assigned' to them, meaning they have first call on the proceeds.

This matter of the tax-free surplus is not, naturally, left to chance, or to the superlative skill of the life company in investing your premiums. The size of the premiums that you pay are set at a level which automatically ensures there is a good 'safety net' built in. Matters would have to be very dire indeed for the policy to fail to produce the sum required for paying off the mortgage.

Most endowment policies are 'with-profits' although there

is an alternative form called 'unit-linked'. A with-profits policy is invested in a mixture of equities, property and gilts; a unit-linked policy can offer the policy holder a choice, between a Managed Fund, which has a similar mixture of investments, or various specialist funds which may invest only in UK equities, for example, or American equities, or fixed interest securities.

Apart from the matter of investment choice, there is a fundamental difference between unit-linked and with-profits policies. With the latter, the life company builds up reserves rather than paying out all the profits as it goes along and uses these reserves in the bad times to smooth out investment returns. A good instance of this has happened this year, in 1988, when several life companies have maintained their levels of bonuses on with-profits policies, despite the stock market crash of 1987.

Bonuses on with-profits policies are the means by which investment profits are allocated, and come in two forms: the reversionary or annual bonus, allocated to all policies once a year, and which is effectively the interest and dividends earned on the underlying investments. Then there is the terminal bonus which is added to the policy once only, right at the end of its life. This represents the underlying capital growth on the investments over the whole period of the policy's life.

In order to set the level of premiums on the policy, lenders insist that only a certain percentage of the current reversionary bonus is taken into account - normally between 80 and 85 per cent. The terminal bonus is ignored altogether. The precise mechanics need not concern the policy holder, though it's important to know that there is such a safety net built in.

With a unit-linked policy, there are no reserves to even out the bad times with the good; the investor is getting his performance 'neat'. Nevertheless, here too, lenders try to ensure a safety margin by making a conservative assumption as to how fast the policy is likely to grow over the term. The usual rate chosen is 7.5 per cent a year. Policies will also have a provision in them enabling the premiums to be raised automatically if, after say ten years, the actual rate of growth achieved has not matched expectations.

How should you go about choosing a policy, if you have decided the endowment route is best for you? There is no easy answer. The majority of people with endowment policies choose – though not perhaps consciously – a with-profits policy. If your mortgage is your major form of saving, this is probably sensible: it is always good to have a bedrock of a fairly conservative scheme as the foundation for your investments.

But how do you choose from the ninety-odd companies which offer with-profits policies? The first thing to be said is that quotations provided by the companies themselves are of very little help indeed. Table 6 gives an example of a life company quotation for an endowment mortgage. The weasel word appears on the right hand side: '*If* the company earns a net investment return of 10.75% per annum. . .' There is absolutely no guarantee that it will, nor is there any indication whether it has managed such a feat in the past. In any case, all life companies must now quote on an identical basis, using the same assumed growth rate. This means that the actual information a quotation is giving you

Table 6
Quotation for a Low-Cost With-Profits Endowment Policy

Male age not exceeding 30;
Mortgage of £25,000 repayable at the end of 25 years;
Guaranteed minimum sum payable on death of £25,000.

The cost (ignoring mortgage interest)	£	The benefits	£
Monthly premium	32.20	At the end of term: at 80 per cent of reversionary bonus projected at current rate	25,000
Total cost of policy over term	9,660.00		
		If the company earns a net investment return of 10.75% per annum	37,218
		Less repayment of mortgage	25,000
		Balance	12,218

Source: *Norwich Union.*
Notes: The projected sum payable will depend on bonuses earned in the future. Bonuses once added cannot be taken away.

is restricted to two things: one, the level of premiums you
have to pay and two, by implication, the size of the hidden
charges on the policy.

It does not tell you whether the company concerned has
a good investment record; for that, the only guide (and that
an inadequate one) is past performance. Do get independent
professional advice if you can. Obviously, no one can know
which company is going to produce the best results in the
future, but a competent insurance broker should be able to
point you to a company with reasonable prospects of being
among the front runners.

Pension Mortgages

A 'pension mortgage' works like an endowment mortgage
– with an extra helping of tax reliefs to spice things up. Most
pension schemes give their members the opportunity to take
out a tax-free cash sum on retirement, and the idea is to use
this sum to pay off your mortgage.

All qualifying pension schemes are supremely favoured by
the taxman. The premiums you pay are fully tax deductible;
the pension fund itself attracts neither income nor capital
gains tax; and on retirement you can 'commute' part of your
pension fund into cash, although the major portion must be
used to provide yourself with a regular income.

There are two major problems with the idea of pension
mortgages. The first is from the lender's point of view. Most
lenders are prepared to accept (though sometimes grudgingly)
that a pension scheme can be an acceptable means of paying off
the mortgage, but many are still fairly wary. If you are in a
'final salary' type pension scheme provided for you by your
employer, many lenders will refuse to accept it. They worry,
for example, that you may be forced into early retirement and
have to accept a much lower pension (and consequently, cash
sum) than you had anticipated.

The rights to a pension policy cannot, by law, be assigned
to anyone else, so the lender is in a fairly vulnerable position,
particularly when you bear in mind he may be lending you
the money not for 25 years, but perhaps 30 or even 35,
until retirement, with no prospect of the capital being repaid
until that point.

Lenders are happier with the idea of personal pensions
– although in truth there is no logical reason why this should

Table 7
Comparison of Costs: Low–Cost Endowment Mortgage versus Pension Mortgage
For a man aged 40 next birthday, taking out a £25,000 mortgage over 25 years, basic-rate taxpayer.

Low-cost endowment	£	Pension	£
1 The costs			
Endowment premium	42.90	Pension premium	74.86
		+ life assurance	10.23
		Net of 25 per cent relief =	63.82
Mortgage interest	160.25	Mortgage interest	
(at 10.25%)		(at 10.25%)	160.25
Total monthly cost	203.15	Total monthly cost	224.07
2 The proceeds			
Endowment policy	45,827.00	Pension policy	147,927.00
Less mortgage	25,000.00	Maximum cash sum	36,982.00
		Less mortgage	25,000.00
Tax-free surplus	20,827.00	Tax-free surplus plus	11,981.75
		Pension for life	14,579 p.a.

Source: *Guardian Royal Exchange*
Note: The low-cost endowment policy illustration assumes bonuses will be added consistently with a net investment return of 10.75% p.a.
The pension policy illustration assumes bonuses will be added consistently with an investment return of 13% p.a.

be so. So if you are self-employed, or are contemplating leaving your company scheme for a new personal pension (see Chapter Seven) then you should have no problems in fixing yourself up with a pension mortgage.

The problem from the borrower's point of view is simply this: that you must not fall into the trap of thinking that just because you have a 'pension mortgage', you are automatically providing yourself with an adequate pension as well as a means of paying off your mortgage. It could well be that you will have to save extra amounts into the pension scheme.

As a very rough rule of thumb, if you are 40 or thereabouts, you should be saving the maximum allowable under Inland Revenue limits – 17.5 per cent of your salary each year – for your pension alone, and not earmark any of it towards paying off the mortgage. This is particularly important if you have made no, or little, pension provision in the past.

But then you can look at it from the opposite point of view as well: a pension mortgage does at least force you to put some money towards a pension - something you might otherwise find hard to do, as jam today is always more alluring than the prospect of jam many years in the future.

Table 7 shows an example of a quotation for a pension mortgage compared with an endowment mortgage. You will notice that the gross outlay on the pension plan is much greater than on the endowment - £85.09 compared to £42.90 in this example. This is because the total pension fund must be a great deal larger at the end of the day, given that the greater part of it must by law be used to buy a pension.

After tax relief, however, that gap is considerably narrowed, and when you look at the benefits, the pension scheme far outweighs the endowment. You will also notice that the assumed rate of growth of the pension plan is higher than the endowment, to reflect the fact the investments are growing tax free.

Which Mortgage Should You Choose?

Repayment, endowment or pension mortgage? As a matter of fact, the majority of home buyers opt for an endowment mortgage these days. When the mortgage rate is relatively low - say, 11.5 per cent or less - the difference in net monthly outlay between a repayment and an endowment mortgage is negligible, particularly when you add on the cost of life assurance to the repayment mortgage. If interest rates rise, however, endowment mortgages become relatively more expensive.

The same principle applies to pension mortgages which are also more expensive than the alternatives, except perhaps for higher rate taxpayers who benefit from proportionately greater tax relief on their pension premiums.

A mortgage is a big fact in anyone's financial life, but it's not the only one. The decision you make must take into account your whole financial circumstances: whether you have any other savings, whether you need to save wholeheartedly for your pension without hanging a mortgage round its neck; whether you think the additional flexibility of a repayment mortgage is going to be important for you in the future.

The size of the mortgage can also have a bearing. If it is

in excess of £30,000 you could consider a 'mixed' mortgage with the first £30,000 backed by an endowment or pension mortgage and the balance on a repayment basis.

My own preference is for an endowment or (where appropriate) pension mortgage; but you must make your own decision.

Interest Rates - Tricks and Treats

There are quoted interest rates, and there are APRs (Annual Percentage Rates) and it wouldn't do to confuse the two. It is easy to become mesmerised by rates if you are shopping around, but remember a mortgage lasts a long time and there's no way of knowing whether one lender will remain marginally cheaper than others throughout the life of the mortgage. In any case, if you are taking out a repayment mortgage, the quoted rate is an inaccurate guide, as different lenders have different systems for charging interest. Look instead at the APR, which all lenders must reveal by law.

You should also keep an eye on the cost (if any) of the mortgage indemnity policy, the arrangement fee, and any other bits of small print: a few lenders, for example, charge an early redemption penalty, others may insist on your taking out a relatively expensive life assurance policy. All this can outweigh the advantage of a lower interest rate.

And as for the mortgage rate itself, most people have variable rate mortgages and adjusting to the up and down of monthly mortgage payments has become a way of life. However as new financial instruments have been devised, lenders have been able to offer fixed rate, or 'cap and collar' mortgages.

Fixed rate mortgage offers are always limited, both as to the amount of money there is to lend on this basis, and the period of time during which you can take it up. From the lender's point of view, the offers are best made when they perceive interest rates on a downward trend, whereas for borrowers, of course, the opposite is true. In any case, the guarantee of the fixed rate is limited, typically to a time–span of one to three years.

A fixed rate mortgage has the advantage that you know where you are for that time; whether you will actually 'win' (in the sense of enjoying a lower rate than the average variable rate over that term) is frankly quite unpredictable.

A 'cap and collar' mortgage is a variation on this theme. Instead of offering a fixed rate, a 'cap and collar' guarantees that the interest rate will not rise above a certain limit – and stipulates also that it will not fall below a lower limit. These are also limited offers, and require the borrower to pay a premium of perhaps several hundred pounds. Sometimes you can get the 'cap' without the 'collar'.

Alternatively, some lenders offer mortgages linked directly to the three-month London Inter Bank Offered Rate (Libor). The lenders charge a fixed margin (typically $3/4$ to 1 per cent) above three month Libor, and the rate is automatically adjusted every three months, according to when the lender has its 'fixing day'.

Libor-linked mortgages would not have been attractive a decade ago, when building societies maintained fairly stable mortgage rates which were often below money market rates; but competition – and the societies' reliance on money market funds for much of their lending – mean the two are moving closer together and there is little to choose between them.

The most recent development on the mortgage scene has been 'equity share' arrangements, where a lender takes some of the future capital appreciation on your property in exchange for charging you a lower interest rate on the mortgage. The schemes are aimed at first-time buyers and are very few and far between at the moment. Several major building societies were considering introducing them in early 1988, and we could see many more such schemes in operation shortly.

Looking After and Improving Your Home
Top of the list must be to insure your home. Fortunately, perhaps, most house buyers do not have the option to live dangerously, as their mortgage lender will insist that proper buildings insurance is taken out (and they will pay the premiums for you, if you fall behind, adding that debt to your mortgage).

Insurance of contents is not compulsory, so if you are prepared to risk all your worldly goods, you can do so. Those with a more realistic, or less ascetic, attitude to their possessions should make sure they are fully insured.

If you decide to make major improvements to your property, the odds are that you will have to borrow the money to do so. Sadly, since the 1988 Budget, these loans no longer qualify for tax relief on the interest.

Nevertheless, the cheapest method of borrowing for improvements is still to get a further advance on your original mortgage. The interest rate should normally be the same as the basic mortgage rate, or perhaps 1 per cent higher, and the term of the further advance is usually set to coincide with the end of the original mortgage term.

Building societies are, however, beginning to promote 'secured personal loans' which can be used for any purpose, including home improvements. The interest rate on these, while attractive compared to banks' personal loans, is considerably higher than the basic mortgage rate. Stick to the further advance on your mortgage if you can. One point to note is that not all of the banks and other specialist mortgage lenders offer a further advance facility, so you should check this out first.

If you are contemplating major changes to your home, you will have to establish first whether planning permission is required. The Department of Environment publishes a free leaflet called *Planning Permission: A Guide for Householders.*

Are improvements a good investment? Not necessarily: some can be positively disastrous. Fake stone cladding is probably the most notorious so-called 'improvement' as it can wreak serious damage on the structure of a house, as well as render it virtually unsellable. Surprisingly, perhaps, swimming pools are not far behind, at least in this country (California may be another matter). Potential buyers can be put off by the cost of upkeep and you are unlikely to recoup the full cost of installation.

It is wise to bear in mind the estate agent's adage: don't have the most expensive house in your street. The actual location of your house is the single most important factor in determining its price. If you live in a street of £50,000 houses, no amount of titivating, at no matter what expense, will make yours worth double that amount.

That said, some improvements are good investments. First, ensure that the property is wind- and weather-proof. Fitted kitchens and bathrooms, fitted wardrobes and a garage will add value to the property. So, it appears, does a loft extension if you can pack in an extra bedroom under the roof. Double glazing does not seem to appeal to many buyers and you would be unlikely to recoup the cost of installation very quickly; cavity wall insulation doesn't do anything for buyers either.

It is difficult to generalise, of course, and sooner or later one steps into the minefield question of good taste. If you are busy improving your house in the hope of making a quick killing, just remember that your idea of a dream home may be another's nightmare!

Further Information
Do it Yourself Conveyancing:
The Legal Side of Buying a House (published by the Consumers' Association)
The Conveyancing Fraud by Michael Joseph (published by the author – 27 Occupation Lane, Woolwich, London SE18)
Buying and Selling a House or Flat by Marjorie Giles (Pan)

General Information on House Purchase and Mortgages:
The Building Societies Association (3 Savile Row, London W1X 1AF) publishes various free booklets on house purchase, mortgages etc. Many building societies issue free literature on all matters concerned with house buying, home improvements and so on.

Diana Wright

4 The Stock Market

Although it used generally to be thought that investing in the stock market was something only indulged in by a rich minority, thanks to the Government's privatisation programme an extraordinary nine million individuals in the UK now hold shares. It is true that many of them hold shares in only one or two companies, rather than a diversified portfolio which spreads the risk widely but, nonetheless, the stock market is being seen by an ever greater number of people as a suitable place to invest part of their long-term savings.

The extraordinary volatility of the stock market demonstrated in 1987, when share prices collapsed with unprecedented savagery, brought home the frequently quoted truth that, unless you are a professional investor, you should only invest in shares money that you can afford to lose if the worst comes to the worst, money that you are not likely to need in a hurry for some emergency and money that you are willing to salt away for many years.

It is possible that the 1987 Crash, which attracted so much publicity, will have put many investors and potential investors off the idea of investing in shares at all. Although all those who held on to shares bought through the Government's privatisation programme were showing profits before stock markets around the world collapsed, many were surprised to find that in a matter of only weeks their shares were worth less than they had originally paid for them. This surprise was all the greater because, in many cases, people had not appreciated the risks inherent in stock market investment; at least part of the blame for this ignorance must lie with the Government's marketing campaign.

It seems sensible, therefore, to ask why anybody should invest in shares at all if they are so risky? The answer has to be that, over the long-term, they have provided a return to investors unparalleled by almost any other sort of investment.

If, as a basic rate taxpayer, you had invested £1,000 in a building society at the beginning of 1946 and left it untouched,

to gather dust and interest ever since, then by the beginning
of 1987 it would have been worth £7,210.

If you had also invested £1,000 in the stock market at the same
time, that money would have grown to almost £84,000, even
after allowing for the depradations of basic rate income tax.

Inflation, of course, ought to be taken into account in such
exercises and it is interesting to see that, whilst the building
society investor would have halved his or her money in real
terms, the investor who bought shares would have wound
up with five-and-a-half times his original stake in real terms.

So what is a share? It is, literally, part of a business. If
a company needs an injection of capital, issuing shares to
investors can be a viable alternative to going to the bank for
the money. Each share gives its holder a stake in the company,
in direct proportion to the number held. Each shareholder is,
in effect, a part owner of the company.

Their shares, however, entitle them to almost nothing.
If the business gets into serious trouble and is wound up,
shareholders are the last to be paid anything. Everybody else
has first call. When the business is doing well, everyone else
still has first call. There is the wages bill, the tax bill, the rates
bill, the bank interest, the interest on any other loans – all these
have to be settled before the shareholders see anything.

If, as the investor hopes, the business is prospering, then
there ought to be plenty left in the kitty after everyone else
has been seen right. If this is the case, the company will
probably pay part of the profits out to investors in the form
of dividends, keeping the rest to plough back into the business to
finance future growth. As the company grows so, one hopes,
will the dividends.

On the whole, investors rarely buy shares because of the
yield received from dividends. Yields on equities, as they
are also known, tend to be below comparable fixed-interest
investments. If the shares are held for a considerable time,
however, yields may rise to quite handsome levels. Marks and
Spencer, for instance, gave its shareholders just over a penny in
dividends back in 1977, which meant investors had a net yield of
just over 3 per cent. It does not sound terribly attractive. However, those shareholders would have held onto their shares not
because of the dividend existing at that time, but because they
hoped that as the company grew, so too would the dividend.

They were justified in that faith. In 1987 M & S paid out 4.5 pence on its shares. Although a seemingly paltry dividend for those buying the shares then, those who had purchased them in 1977 at just 30p would be receiving an income of 15 per cent net on their original stake, or 20 per cent gross.

On top of that, the shares rose six-fold over the period, giving shareholders an eminently satisfactory capital gain as well!

The whole business of dealing in shares has changed considerably over the past few years, in the main because of the transformation wrought by Big Bang, the reorganisation of the Stock Exchange that took place on 27 October 1986. Many of the changes have had an effect only on the big institutional investors, rather than private individuals. Yet all investors have been affected by the fact that the old trading floor of the Stock Exchange no longer exists.

In its place is a screen-and-telephone market. When you rang a stockbroker to ask a price in a particular share preparatory to dealing, he used to send a dealer into the stock market to ask all the share wholesalers, or jobbers, what price they were prepared to deal at. Now, he has on his desk a TOPIC screen, a video display unit on which are shown the prices made by all the wholesalers, or market-makers, in each share. Your broker can easily locate where he can buy your shares most cheaply or where he can get the best price for them if you are selling. To carry out the order, he need only to pick up the telephone and ring the market-maker. Within seconds, the deal is done. That, at any rate, is the theory. In practice, the system works a good deal less effectively at times of market turmoil.

One advantage of this new system is that it is just as easy for the provincial stockbroking firms to place orders as it is for those firms based within the Square Mile. Under the old system, it could be a positive disadvantage to be based away from London. Now, it does not matter at all where a stockbroker is based. In fact, because of lower office and staff costs, it is frequently the case that regional stockbrokers charge their customers less for dealing than the bigger City outfits.

That is the other major change brought about by Big Bang. Brokers used to be compelled to charge exactly the same to all clients. Anyone dealing in shares up to £7,000 in value would have paid 1.65 per cent in commission. Now brokers are free

Example of a Contract Note Showing a Share Purchase

Time	Quantity	Stock	Price	Consideration
1:15	500	Megacorp Ordinary	350	1750.00
			Transfer Stamp	9.00
			Commission 1.5%	26.25
			VAT at 15%	3.93
			Contract levy	0.80
			Total	1789.98

Notes. All contract notes should show the time at which the deal was transacted which will help in the event of any dispute.

Stamp duty is levied at 0.5%, rounded up to the nearest 50 pence.

This deal assumes that the broker's minimum commission is below £26. If it is above, then the commission charge will obviously be greater, increasing the total cost of the transaction.

Contract levy: every sale or purchase of shares over £1,000 attracts a flat levy of 80p.

---

to charge whatever they like and, as a result, rates vary widely from firm to firm. It is important that investors check not only what percentage commission is going to be charged, but also what minimum the broker sets on any deal. This is very important, particularly for smaller orders. It is all very well going to a firm which only levies 1.5 per cent, but if you are going to be charged a minimum of £30 or £40 and your share purchase or sale is relatively small, you would be far better off going somewhere where you might be able to deal for as little as £15 or £20.

Commission is not the only charge you will find when your stockbroker sends you a contract note. VAT will be levied on it and, if you are making a purchase, you will also have to pay a half per cent of the cost of the shares in stamp duty. A contract note, confirming your order, should arrive within a day or so and will be proof that the deal has been carried out. (See example above.)

I ought to point out that commission is only payable once shares have started trading. If you buy shares in a new issue such as a privatisation, filling out a form in a newspaper and sending off your cheque with it, then you will not have to pay any commission or stamp duty, simply the value of the shares.

Bear in mind that the buying price of a share is always different from the selling price, the difference between them being the 'spread'. This spread, charged by the market-makers, is the way in which they earn their income. It is not shown in most newspapers, except for *The Times*. They prefer instead merely to show the mid-price of the shares. However, you should take the spread into account when considering whether your investments are showing a profit or not, as you should brokers' commission. In order to cover commission and spreads, a share's mid-price may have to climb 5 or 6 per cent or more, before you begin to see any profit.

The Stock Exchange operates on a fortnightly Account system. All deals with any one broker taking place within the two weeks (occasionally three) of an Account Period are amalgamated. If, for instance, you have made one purchase of £2,000 and a sale of £1,500, you will merely have to write a cheque to your broker for £500, the net balance. This amount will be due on what is known as Settlement Day. As will be made clear on the contract note, Settlement Day is the second Monday after an account closes. On that day the broker should pay you if you are a net seller, or you should make sure you have paid him if you have bought shares.

If a buyer, the broker will arrange that the share certificate with your name on it will eventually be forwarded by the company and that their register of shareholders is amended accordingly. Keep all your share certificates in a safe place. Although it is possible to replace them, it involves a considerable degree of inconvenience.

If you have sold shares then, along with the contract note, you will be sent a Sold Transfer Form by your broker. You sign this and despatch the relevant certificates with it to him. He will handle all the rest of the administrative process for you.

The actual mechanics of dealing in stocks and shares is really terribly simple, particularly as it can be carried out over the telephone and by post without your ever needing to meet your stockbroker in person.

Finding a stockbroker, however, is not such a simple matter. There were hopes that Big Bang would see a surge in firms willing to take on private client business. But the increase in costs faced by stockbrokers in re-equipping with new technology and the hike in salaries for staff meant that small, private client business ceased to be cost-effective at many institutions, particularly as their back office administration procedures

would appear to be a good deal less efficient than might
have been desired.

Many of the simple 'deal-only' services brought in soon
after Big Bang, were cut back or dropped, whilst stockbrokers
offering the more traditional stockbroking services were in
some cases reluctant to take on new clients. So, finding a broker
may involve a degree of perseverence on your part. As with
finding a lawyer or plumber, a recommendation from a friend
or colleague may be the best way of starting out. However,
not everybody knows somebody with a broker. If that is the
case, you will probably find some stockbroking firms listed in
your Yellow Pages. These days many broking firms also advertise for business in various financial publications. Ring some
of them, and see how helpful they are.

You can also obtain, from the Stock Exchange, a booklet
called 'An Introduction to the Stock Market'. Although very
basic, it does have a useful list of those stockbroking firms willing to take on new private clients, together with the areas in
which those firms operate. The booklet might be a useful starting point in your search for a broker.

These days the banks and building societies are becoming
interested in offering a share-dealing service and many people
prefer to deal with institutions with which they are already
familiar, rather than some remote stockbroker. The quality of
service is rather variable, however, and in many cases you are
merely putting a middle man between yourself and the stockbroker, for all share transactions must go through a member of
the Stock Exchange. Most of the High Street banks now own
stockbroking firms as a result of the transformation wrought
by Big Bang and the facilities they are offering are steadily
improving. Barclays' recent introduction of 'Barclayshare'
brings them even closer to most people's idea of a traditional
stockbroking firm.

Some investors like to make their own investment decisions,
ringing up their broker simply in order to give their buying or
selling orders. If this is your preferred way of trading, then
one of the cheaper 'deal-only' services may well be for you. If
you need advice and like to talk investment ideas through with
somebody beforehand, then the more usual broking service
might be preferable. Although a little more expensive, your
stockbroker is likely to have a good feel for the way the stock

market is moving and some background knowledge of some of the more interesting shares. Remember, though, that with over 3,000 shares traded on the UK stock market, his knowledge cannot possibly be comprehensive.

Others prefer to hand over their portfolios to their stock-brokers, or even their banks, to look after them. Here, there are two services that might be considered. An 'advisory' service is one under which you agree parameters for your investments beforehand. The manager of your portfolio will suggest possible investments to you, but the final decisions rest with you. Those who want to leave everything to their advisers will opt for the 'discretionary' service, with the manager making all the decisions and acting upon them without having to refer back to you.

No matter what kind of service you opt for with your stockbroker or bank, the new Financial Services Act insists that your adviser provides you with a client agreement letter to sign at the beginning of your relationship. This long and rather complex document will attempt to set out the business relationship between you, explaining the nature of the service provided and the sort of investment category into which you fit. It remains to be seen how effective this piece of bureaucracy will prove in the event of problems arising.

If you do want to have a hand in your own investment decisions, you will quickly realise that with so many shares quoted on the London stock market, choosing between them is not an easy task. In fact, it can prove so bewildering that many novices might be tempted to give up before they start.

The price of shares doesn't remain constant, but changes not only from day to day, but even from minute to minute within that day. Why? Quite simply, this is in reaction to the movements of buyers and sellers of the shares in the marketplace who are making investment decisions based upon what they perceive to be the attractions or disadvantages of particular shares.

It is a common fallacy to assume that a share with a low price is 'cheap' and one with a high price 'expensive'. If that were all there were to investment analysis, there would be far fewer people working in the City than there are. Analysis boils down, in the end, to 'How much per share?' - How much profit is the company making on each share? What are its assets per share? What is the dividend per share? These and other blood-quickening questions are meat and drink for investment analysis.

The importance of looking at investment sums in this way can be demonstrated by the decision of the Trustee Savings Bank to raise £1.5 billion from the public. They opted to do so by selling 1,500 million shares at a pound each. Many people said they bought the shares because £1 sounded 'cheap'. Yet TSB would have raised exactly the same amount if they had made the shares 50p each and issued twice as many, or if they had made them £2 each and sold 750 million. Altering the number of shares would have altered the amount of profits per share, dividend per share, and all the other investment sums. But in the eyes of the professional investment analysts, their calculations would have given them exactly the same end result no matter how many shares were issued, providing the amount of money raised was the same.

This practice of looking at investment in terms of each share is mirrored in the sections of the quality newspapers devoted to quoting the prices of shares traded on the stock market. Here are given not only the year's high and low for each share, but also such esoteric measures as the PE ratio, the yield and dividend cover.

The paper may show the actual dividend paid out. If so, it is important to note whether this is a gross or net figure. Dividends arrive with basic rate tax already paid on your behalf by the company. Higher rate taxpayers must declare them when they make their annual return and will have to pay additional tax. Non-taxpayers may claim it back.

Even if the figure for the dividend isn't given in your paper, the yield almost certainly will be. This has already been partially explained. The yield, which is calculated on the gross payout to make comparison with other investments easier, will obviously vary from day to day as the price of the shares varies. As the price increases, so the dividend becomes a smaller proportion of the current share price and the yield diminishes. A price fall will see the yield increase.

A company will usually pay out its dividends to its share-holders twice a year, announcing the size of the payments when it unveils its interim and its final results. The ability of a company to pay dividends to its shareholders will depend on the success it has had in trading. Firms will be reluctant to give shareholders everything that is left in the kitty, preferring instead to plough some of the money back into the business. However, it is useful to know how much *could* have been paid to shareholders had the company chosen to do so. The figure for Dividend Cover will show just how many times it was able to pay the dividend. The higher the number, the greater the firm's earnings are in relation to the dividend payout and the 'safer' shareholders' income is. A cover of just 1.0 indicates that a company has paid out all of its available earnings in the form of a dividend, leaving nothing in the coffers for a rainy day.

Although yield is one of the main factors an investor will consider when weighing up a potential share investment, the potential for capital gain will obviously be another. Although it is very difficult to generalise here, it is probable that the fastest-growing companies, in terms of their profits and earnings, will also be the ones with the fastest-growing share prices. Growth businesses tend to pay out very little in the way of dividends, particularly in their early years, so shareholders hope instead for capital gain to reward them.

It is useful to examine the earnings a company produces on each of its shares, not only in the current year, but also over the past few years. Are the earnings – in essence what is left for the shareholders after everybody else has had what is coming to them – on a steadily rising trend? Is the trend likely to continue? Can you find an explanation for any hiccups in the trend?

Locating those companies with good track records, however, may be no use if their merits are already fully appreciated by every other investor under the sun. So we need a way of measuring the 'cheapness' or 'expensiveness' of any share. The most common way of doing this is through the Price-Earnings Ratio, a calculation which considers the earnings the company is making as a proportion of the current share price. If a company is making 10 pence for its shareholders on each share and those shares are priced in the market at 150p, then the PE ratio would be 15. You should compare this figure with other companies involved in similar businesses. The higher the PE, the more highly investors collectively 'rate' that company and the higher the growth they are likely to be expecting.

You will notice as you look through the columns of PE ratios that some sectors of the market have markedly different PEs than others. Banks, have very low PEs whereas food retailers or advertising agencies may have much higher PEs.

Professional investors are looking, not only at the current PE, but at the prospective figure. They will have produced an estimate for the profits a company will make this year and next and worked out how much the PE will drop as the earnings increase. The faster the growth is generally reckoned to be, the higher the current PE is likely to be. You should realise that the figure in the newspaper is based on last year's profits. It may be that the company in which you are interested is going to announce profits tomorrow. If earnings are sharply higher, then the figure for the PE ratio will drop, assuming an unchanged share price.

PEs are not an absolute tool, but a relative one. Investors using them should be on the lookout for companies which have lower than average PEs but which they believe will have a growth rate above the average for that sector. If you are right, and the profits are above general expectations, then the share price is likely to rise after the announcement of the company's results. If the market then becomes convinced, as you are, that it has been underestimating the potential for growth in that company, then it may decide a higher PE is in order and the share price will climb until the adjustment is made.

In essence, a high PE indicates an expectation for high growth. Be aware, however, that if investors' hopes for that growth is not justified, a rapid down-rating of that company could occur, involving a sharp drop in the share price.

For those who do want to do a little of their own research work, the Report and Accounts that each company has to produce every year will prove invaluable. This is available free on request either from the company itself or from its registrars.

One of the most important things any investor must do when contemplating putting some of his savings into the stock market is to spread his risk - unless he actually prefers to speculate on merely one or two shares. Some stockbrokers, given a relatively small amount to handle by clients, will divert them into a pooled investment vehicle such as a unit or investment trust, as the only reasonable way to achieve a relatively wide exposure (20 shares or more) with a small investment. Chapter Five goes into greater detail about the different types of vehicle available. Many investors use unit or investment trusts to give them exposure to main line shares in the UK, or to overseas markets where considerable expertise is needed to invest, while keeping a smaller part of their funds for speculating in shares directly.

Tax is something that must be considered with all forms of investment, and the stock market is no exception. Dividends, the income from shares, are treated like much other income. They arrive with basic rate income tax having already been deducted. Attached to the cheques are tax credits, showing the taxman exactly how much has been paid on your behalf to the Revenue. All taxpayers will need to show these payments on their tax returns, with higher rate payers being liable for paying the excess amount eventually.

However, unlike building society or bank interest, non-taxpayers can reclaim the tax paid in their name.

The other form of tax which might trouble you (apart from the stamp duty payable on your share purchases) is Capital Gains Tax. This is currently a tax at your marginal income tax rate on the net gains you realise from your investments, and many investors go to great lengths to avoid paying it. However, there is a substantial threshold on CGT of £5,000. This is set so high that the majority of investors will never be troubled by CGT. A portfolio of £20,000 would need to rise 25 per cent, and then be sold within the same tax year, in order to incur CGT. For most people, the tax will probably be an aim, rather than something to avoid!

In the light of this, the introduction of Personal Equity Plans by the Chancellor of the Exchequer seem a little peculiar. They allow individuals to contribute up to £3,000 a year, or £250 a month, to a scheme managed by a registered Plan Manager. This is then channelled into buying shares or, possibly, unit or investment trusts. Investors need to hold their PEPs for one calendar year after the year of setting up in order to qualify for the tax benefits, which give investors relief from both income tax and capital gains tax.

For most investors, it is only the freedom from income tax that is likely to be of interest and this, unfortunately, is frequently more than offset by the management charges levied by the plan managers. PEPs need to be a *very* long-term investment for many investors to reap any benefit from the largesse of the Chancellor. PEPs are a cumbersome and unwieldy animal and, strangely, the one thing they are not is 'Personal'. Investors can not effectively manage their own investments in a PEP.

Another tax concession is available to those who invest in a Business Expansion Scheme project. The BES was set up to assist with providing capital for young businesses and allows those who hold their shares for a minimum of five years to write off their investments against income tax. This is a rather better idea, although all investors should remember that tax relief is no good if the underlying investment is not sound. It is useless being able to write your investment off against tax if you have to write it off altogether. BES, by its very nature, is the riskier end of equity investment.

Despite the advances made in the drive towards wider share ownership over the past few years, the trend towards having our savings managed by the big institutions - the pension funds and insurance companies - has not yet been reversed, and may well never be. In 1957 individuals owned 66 per cent of all shares quoted in the UK, while the institutions had only 18 per cent. Today the position has been exactly reversed, with the institutions holding an estimated 66 per cent of equities and individuals 20 per cent or less.

These fund managers wield immense power and, although it is ultimately our money that is being invested on our behalf in the stock market, we have very little control over it.

Whatever decisions you make with regard to investment on the stock market you should realise that, through your pensions schemes and insurance arrangements, a large part of your savings may already be invested there. Although this inevitably involves a greater degree of risk than with more straightforward fixed-interest investment, one must also realise that such responsible groups would never be risking the funds entrusted to them in this way if they truly believed that the stock market was nothing more than a casino.

It is not. It is a sensible place to invest part of your savings for the long-term, with past experience telling us that, over time, you will receive a handsome return. On the other hand, risking money you can ill afford to lose on short-term gambles in the market may be fun, but you should fully appreciate the possible consequences before you plunge in.

Simon Rose

5 Spreading the Risk

Gambling or Investing?

Consider tossing a coin for 10p a throw; guess correctly and your money's returned with another 10p. Pure gambling with the odds on winning in the hands of statistical probability. Toss an infinite number of times and you would only break even. To win you must stop while you are ahead, but hit a losing streak and you may well run out of capital before achieving the goal.

Investment, by contrast, may be likened to partially loading the coins; achieving a bias by assessing each opportunity and minimising the risks involved. You won't always win but the odds may be tilted in your favour.

Portfolio Risk

The first consideration in any portfolio is security, best achieved by imagining a hypothetical pyramid. Cash deposits represent the firm foundations: money in the bank or building society instant access accounts. On these are built a broad base of 'notice' deposits; money, which if required, can be retrieved in a matter of weeks or months. These support gilt investments, involving more risk; prices vary with supply and demand, although there is a guaranteed final redemption figure. Higher up come layers of equity investments, all along ensuring that the higher we travel, the higher the risk, and so less money is allocated; unless, of course, a particular bias is desired – portfolios amounting to several hundred thousand pounds will probably be slanted towards equities. The pinnacle represents pure gamble. Investors must decide for themselves how high to build, according to their assets, financial requirements and ability to take the strain – the latter's important, since it is silly to invest past the point at which you begin to worry.

Limited Loss Investments

At the base of our hypothetical pyramid are 'limited loss' investments – return of capital plus a little extra – restricting the down-side risk to the unlikely event of bank or building society

collapse (and even then there is an industry lifeboat); erosion
of purchasing power by inflation; and the 'lost opportunity' of
securing a higher return by investing the capital elsewhere.

Once we reach equity investments, we begin to put capital
at risk, the whole of an investment being susceptible to adverse
movement in share prices - witness the events of October
1987. That said, losses can be minimised by considering the
risks involved.

Specific and Market Risk

Stock market prices are guided by supply and demand, under
the influence of a broad range of economic factors, some of
which remain specific to one company, or industry; others
affect the whole stock market. The former, or specific risk, as it
is sometimes called, may be reduced by diversification across
a broad range of companies and industries. By avoiding stock
concentration in similar or dependent industries, gains in one
area should overcome losses in another. The broader the
spread, the lower the specific risk; fifteen to twenty holdings
is the accepted minimum for a balanced portfolio.

Although market risk is unavoidable, it can be controlled,
given that some companies are more sensitive to macro-
economic factors than others. Basic foodstuffs, for example,
tend to sell, whatever the economic climate. Similarly, in
a falling market, growth stocks will probably fall faster than
income shares on the premise that 'growth' implies potential
and reflects a company reinvesting present profit to establish
itself. Companies with a history of steadily rising dividends
are, probably, at a more financially secure stage of their
development.

Both specific and market risk should be considered when
establishing an equity portfolio; it is not just the quantity
of stock that is essential; diversity and quality are equally as
important.

Pooled Investments

Direct equity investment is fine if you know what you are
doing, have sufficient capital, and time to check performance.
Chapter Four has dealt with this in detail but if you remain
uncertain perhaps pooled investments are the better choice.

Given the relatively high price of blue chip shares and
the proportionately higher fees charged by stockbrokers on
small transactions, £10,000 nowadays buys only a limited

share selection. Buying overseas shares creates more of a problem, not only in the purchase but in acquiring sufficient quality background information on which to base investment decisions. Pooled investments are a way round this problem. Fund managers have access to a wealth of information, some of it gleaned first-hand from the companies concerned. In return for a relatively small outlay, investors benefit from the performance of a broad range of companies. Several options are open; in this section we cover unit trusts, unitised insurance funds, investment trusts and Personal Equity Plans (PEPs).

Before looking at each in detail, let us first consider their respective tax implications; after all, what is good for the basic rate taxpayer is often highly unsuitable for those paying higher rate tax.

Tax and Unitised Investments
Capital Gains Tax

Unit and investment trusts are treated similarly for tax purposes. Neither are themselves liable to capital gains tax (except on gilt dealings). Liability passes to the investors where the usual rules apply: gains will be added to all others realised by the investor during the current tax year and the excess over the investor's annual exemption limit is taxed as income, after deducting indexation allowance (based on changes in Retail Prices Index over the period since March 1982 during which the trust was held) and any allowable losses. Losses incurred during the year of assessment (not necessarily from other unit trust holdings) may be offset against gains of the same year; losses carried forward may be used only to reduce gains to the exemption limit.

Since authorised unit trusts are liable to capital gains tax on gilt dealings, gilts are often best purchased direct; either through a stockbroker, or across the Post Office counter.

By contrast, unitised insurance funds are themselves liable to capital gains tax and this is normally allowed for in the price of the units. Investors should note, therefore, that although they are not personally liable, gains tax has been paid which they may well have otherwise avoided by the gain falling within their annual exemption limit.

Income Tax

Unit trusts and investment trusts are liable to corporation tax only on 'unfranked' income (primarily overseas investments) since the tax on 'franked' income (UK share dividends) has already been paid by the companies owning the underlying shares. As a result, investment trust share dividends are paid net of basic rate tax; so, too, are the distribution payments made by unit trusts, with accumulation unit holders getting a credit slip. Higher rate taxpayers are liable to any excess between the higher rate of tax and basic rate. Non-taxpayers can reclaim the tax already paid, from the Inland Revenue.

With insurance funds the situation is confused by the funds being part of the insurance company's life business. Dividend income is rolled-up inside the fund and the whole of the proceeds available to basic rate taxpayers free of further liability, even on early encashment. Higher rate taxpayers, however, should heed whether the policy is 'qualifying' or 'non-qualifying'.

On qualifying (regular premium) policies the whole of the proceeds are available free of income tax, provided the policy is maintained for ten years, or three-quarters of the intended term, if this is less. Earlier encashment incurs a liability at 15 per cent, the difference between 40 per cent and 25 per cent, the higher rate of income tax and basic rate. 'Top-slicing' relief is available, allowing withdrawals of up to 5 per cent of the original investment to be taken each year, otherwise relief is rolled-up; policies encashed after six years, for example, are eligible for 30 per cent relief; the full allowance coming after twenty years.

On single premium investments (non-qualifying policies) any encashment is liable to higher rate income tax, although again, top-slicing relief is available.

Life assurance premium relief is not available on regular premium policies issued after March 1984 and has never been available on single premium policies.

The 'heavy' bits behind us, we can now look at each vehicle in detail.

Unit Trusts

Units trusts are not companies in their own right but portfolios written under trust for the investors (unit holders) and managed on a day-to-day basis by a fund manager, according to strict guidelines set out in an initial trust deed. Divergence from the trust deed requires consent of the trustee, who is usually a clearing bank. Investors are invited to purchase units in the trust at a price directly reflecting the value of the trust's underlying assets. The trust is divided into a number of equal units, the overall value of the fund at any given time being the product of the unit price and the number of units issued. Unlike company shares, the only market in unit trusts is between the investors and the fund manager.

When demand rises, additional units are issued to match the incoming money and so the value of each unit in relation to the total value of the fund remains unchanged. The reverse holds true when existing investors sell units (back to the fund manager) and the value of the fund contracts.

Bid Prices, Offer Prices

Unit trusts are dealt in two prices: the offer price, at which the investors are invited to buy units; and a lower bid price, at which the fund manager will buy them back. The difference between the two prices is known as the bid–offer spread and includes an initial fee of about 5 per cent, stamp duty at 0.5 per cent, dealing and administration expenses and a 'rounding' element; totalling, at worst, 13 per cent, though typically 6.5 per cent, either down from the maximum offer price, or up from the minimum bid price. Gilt trusts often have a far narrower spread, reflecting the lower dealing costs associated with gilt trans-actions.

Historically, fund managers were able to keep the spread to around 6.5 per cent by trading on their own account. Rather than liquidating part of the underlying portfolio to match repurchases, they held the units themselves for a limited period. In a rising market, the fund manager could pocket extra profit by holding the units and then selling them when the share price had risen - the famous 'box' profits. In a falling market, however, stock on their hands was the last thing fund managers wanted and the trust swiftly shifted to a 'bid basis' - the bid price being quoted at the lowest permitted level to discourage potential sellers and justified as protecting those investors remaining in the fund. Given the potential 13 per cent bid–offer spread, any switch to a bid basis could wipe up to 5 per cent off a trust's performance at a stroke. Without knowing the net asset value of the underlying securities, investors could only guess that a change of basis had occurred. In effect, fund managers manipulated prices to make additional profits in a rising market and, to some extent, covered themselves when markets turned down; a practice long-accepted by the industry watchdog, the Department of Trade and Industry (DTI).

Whatever the rights and wrongs of this practice - the unit trust companies argue that it did not harm unit holders' interests, but others are not so sure. A great practical difficulty with this method of pricing emerged during the 1987 crash. Because markets were falling so fast - on some days, hundreds of points came off the index in the matter of an hour or so - unit trust companies simply could not keep pace in revaluing their portfolios to establish the price at which unit holders could deal.

The result, in some cases, was that investors found for all practical purposes they simply could not cash their units in, for a week or more. An alternative method, forward pricing, has been suggested by the DTI, to be policed by the new industry watchdog, the Securities and Investment Board. This eliminates the risk-free 'box' profits, but it also means that unit holders have to deal 'blind', not knowing the price they have paid (or sold at) until after the deal has gone through.

From 1 July 1988, unit trust managers have the choice of basis on which to value their funds. Historic prices are calculated daily and the trustees notified within two hours. Unless markets move exceptionally the historic prices hold until the next valuation and the bid-offer spread is constant too. Members of the public can, however, insist on a forward price, if quoted an historic price, but not vice versa. Perhaps for the long-term investor, it matters little. But if you are the sort of investor who likes being active, aggressively switching between different funds, then this is an issue you should keep your eye on.

Apart from the initial charge, which is incorporated in the bid-offer spread, the only other charge borne by investors is the annual management fee, ranging from 1 per cent plus VAT on UK trusts to 1.5 per cent plus VAT on some

overseas-invested trusts, reflecting the higher dealing costs
involved. Annual fees are usually charged out of the dividend income produced by the underlying securities. Some
'high yield' trusts enhance income by charging annual fees
to capital growth. Check before investing.

Purchasing Units

Prices are quoted daily in the financial press. Unit trusts
may be purchased by: returning a coupon from the daily
press; ordering over the telephone (bearing in mind that a
verbal contract exists and the conversation will have been
recorded); or through a stockbroker, financial adviser or bank
manager, who receive 3 per cent of the initial charge as
commission for their guidance. Going direct will not save
on commission. In fact, some brokers may even split their
commission with investors to attract new business. The
only other savings are from special discounts offered by
the managers as an incentive - often when a new trust
is launched. The discount is usually up to 1.5 per cent
depending on the amount invested. Switching discounts of
between 2 per cent and 4 per cent are sometimes offered
when investors reinvest the proceeds of a sale of units
in another of the company's trusts; and you can always
try bargaining with the managers when investing, say,
£20,000 or more.

Two types of unit are usually on offer: accumulation,
on which the dividend income accrued on the underlying
securities is automatically reinvested to purchase additional
units; and income units, from which the investor receives
the income payments by way of half-yearly distribution.
Overseas trusts may pay only annually, while some income
trusts pay quarterly or even monthly.

Around six weeks prior to the distribution date is the
accounting date, before which any income accrued in the fund
since the previous distribution will be reflected in the trust's
quoted market price. Such units are deemed 'cum-dividend'
and with ownership comes the entitlement to the forthcom-
ing payment. In the period between the accounting and the
distribution dates, units are offered 'ex-dividend', the fall in
the offer price matching the amount of the net distribution
about to be paid and compensating the new unit holder for
the loss of that payment.

So much for the technical chores; let us see what is on offer.

Choosing a Trust
The unit trust industry has mushroomed over the past six years from around £5 billion under management in early 1981, to over £40 billion by January 1988. There are currently 160 management companies offering over 1,100 unit trusts, with more coming onto the market at a rate of ten a month.

Deciding between unit trusts comes back to risk management. To assist, the Unit Trust Association (UTA) has agreed seventeen sectors, each defining a particular investment area and therefore, to some extent, the risks involved. The current list, along with the number of entrants at the beginning of 1988, is:

UK General	100	Commodity & Energy	31
UK Growth	154	International Growth	144
UK Equity Income	125	International Income	53
UK Mixed Income	24	North America	116
Gilt & FI Income	44	Europe	101
Gilt & FI Growth	11	Far East & Pacific	78
Finance & Property Shares	18	Japan	62
Investment Trust Units	9	Australia	17
Managed	10	**TOTAL** at 1 Jan 1988:	1,097

Trusts in the UK General sector often have holdings in 100 or more companies, thus minimising the specific risk and controlling market risk. Typical names include Allied Dunbar Asset Value, Barclays Unicorn General, M&G General, and Mercury Blue Chip. All the large trust management groups offer a trust in this sector, usually ideal for the first-timer.

By contrast, UK Growth trusts trade under a variety of resplendent titles: Smaller Companies, Recovery, Special Situations, or sometimes just 'Growth' (though only rarely!). Selection involves scrutiny of the individual portfolios, since although specific risk is reduced by stock number, market risk may be relatively high through over-specialisation; a preponderance of smaller companies, for example.

The UK Equity Income sector tends to be inhabited by relatively low-risk trusts and Mixed Income is even safer, as it will have high fixed-interest holdings - gilts, preference stock and convertibles. The two gilt sectors offer the lowest risk ratings but in turn offer the lower rewards.

International unit trusts are relatively low risk investments, since holdings are spread over a variety of markets, with a high proportion in blue chips. That said, a Malaysian blue chip will probably be the equivalent in size of an American smaller company.

Obviously, the fund manager will be party to a wealth of overseas information not available to the private investor; some acquired firsthand from regular trips abroad, some gleaned from local representatives and mutual arrangements with foreign investment houses.

Currency fluctuation poses an additional risk to all overseas investments and although there are various ways to 'hedge' currency exposure, authorised unit trusts are (normally) restricted to back-to-back loans – investment trusts have more leeway and can sell foreign currency forward using futures and options contracts. Back-to-back loans involve the fund manager borrowing, say, dollars from the London office of a US bank – using the assets of the trust as collateral – converting the loan into sterling and placing it on deposit to earn interest. When the time comes to sell the trust's dollar-denominated holdings, the manager will be switching both ways between the two currencies – dollars, from the sales of investments, into pounds; and pounds into dollars when repaying the loan. If 100 per cent hedged the two transactions will cancel one another out. Obviously, the trust manager has to pay interest on the dollar loan. Depending on how sterling moves against the dollar, the interest on the deposit may be greater than the interest paid on the dollar loan: if it is, the fund manager makes an additional profit; if not, the exercise may prove expensive. Trusts vary considerably in the extent to which they hedge currency exposure. Only Gartmore Hedged American is consistently 100 per cent hedged; many managers consider the exercise too expensive.

Specific country unit trusts involve a higher risk than their UK counterparts and particularly those investing in the highly volatile Pacific Basin economies – Singapore, Malaysia, Hong Kong, South Korea and Taiwan – and the smaller European stock exchanges such as Belgium, Holland, Italy and Spain.

Managed trusts are a relative newcomer (October 1986), designed for unit trust first-timers by investing across a range of trusts within a single management group. By and large they have failed to attract significant new money as performance has been relatively poor.

When investing in more than one unit trust, the pyramid rule applies; financial involvement should reduce with increasing risk.

Wider Range Investments

Negotiations are at present underway between the Department of Trade & Industry, the Securities & Investment Board and the Unit Trust Association to introduce wider investment powers for unit trusts. Of these, money market instrument trusts (low risk) are being welcomed by the industry, but commodity futures and options trusts certainly are not. Both are exceedingly high risk. Moves are also afoot to allow trusts direct investment in property; at present they are restricted to holding shares in property companies. Also mooted is the possibility of being allowed to borrow up to 10 per cent of a trust's holdings - even though such 'gearing' would increase the risk factor - and reduce the number of required portfolio holdings from 20 to 16, thereby increasing specific risk. A final decision on these points is expected sometime soon.

Overall, unit trusts are suitable for anyone prepared to take on the additional risk over that offered by capital secure investments, in pursuit of a higher return.

Single or Regular Payments

The minimum investment in unit trusts is usually £500: some groups require £1,000; a few will accept £250. Most major companies offer a regular savings alternative, requiring a minimum commitment of £20 a month or thereabouts.

Whenever regular savings plans are mentioned, the phrase 'pound-cost averaging' is never far away. Spending a set regular amount on buying units entails buying more units when the price is low than when it is high. Assuming a rising market, the average price paid for the units is less than the average market price over the period. In fact, the bigger the fluctuations in the prices at which units are bought, the lower the average purchase cost will be relative to the average unit price.

The only drawback with regular savings plans is that investors are usually restricted to their initial choice of trust until the value of their holdings equals the minimum lump-sum investment required by that trust. Effectively, you could be tied down for several years, the only hope of switching being to cash-in the units and start afresh.

Insurance Funds

Although close relations to unit trusts, insurance funds differ in that the underlying assets are part of an insurance company's life fund. As such, investment is only available through a life assurance policy. For investment purposes, the attendant life cover is kept to an absolute minimum, typically 101 per cent of the current bid value of the units held.

Fund prices are quoted daily in the financial press. The majority of life offices charge an initial fee of 5 per cent reflected in a spread between the bid and offer prices of the units, and an annual management charge of between 1 per cent and 1.5 per cent levied monthly. Several companies operate a single price system, but impose a charge on surrender during the first few years, or allocate less than 100 per cent of the investment to units.

For those companies that operate a bid-offer spread, the unit allocation should be close on 100 per cent; on sums over £5,000, 100 per cent is likely and allocations of up to 105 per cent are available to investors under the age of 40 placing, say £20,000 or more. Be especially careful to look out for 'capital' units on regular premium plans. These are issued only during the first year, sometimes two years, of a plan's intended lifespan and receive a restricted unit allocation, typically 95 per cent. Thereafter, 'accumulation' units are offered with a full 100 per cent (or more) unit allocation.

Like unit trusts, investment may be by single premium (typically £1,000) or regular premium (minimum £25 a month on maximum allocation [investment] plans); and either direct or through a financial intermediary who will receive 5 per cent commission. Two per cent more than on unit trusts, so expect a bit of pressure from the likely lads! Several offices such as Equitable Life and London Life do not pay commission and, as a consequence, are seldom mentioned by brokers.

The choice of investment funds is currently broader than for unit trusts and includes currency and property funds and also a cash or deposit fund, which can be a useful bolt-hole if other investments are looking dicey.

Given the economies involved, there is a growing tendency

for unitised life funds to invest either wholly, or partially, in unit trusts. Most links are in-house, although Clerical Medical invests wholly in the eponymous unit trusts managed by Fidelity. Royal Heritage and Skandia Life have gone further than most; Skandia holding the record with over 150 insurance funds linked to externally managed unit trusts. As with unit trusts, choice involves assessment of risk and the same rules apply.

The main advantage of insurance funds over unit trusts is the freedom to switch investments between the underlying funds, for low or no charge and without incurring a liability to capital gains tax. Most companies allow at least one free switch a year and charge a nominal fee – of around £15 – on subsequent transfers.

Broker-Managed Funds

Broker-managed funds are simply unitised insurance funds, underwritten (and the assets owned) by an insurance company on behalf of a named intermediary, who is free to sell a range of own-label products investing in the fund.

The arrangement is mutually beneficial: the life office gains through increased business; the broker benefits administratively. Investors, too, should benefit (at least in theory). The two-tier management structure should mean that the life company chooses the initial stocks in its in-house range of funds, then the broker selects the best-performing funds for his portfolio. Moreover, the resultant broker fund can be geared towards specific client aims: income, growth, level of risk. How effectively this is done, however, depends on the broker's skills.

Broker Choice

The majority of broker-managed funds are less than £1m in size. Insurance company managed funds tend to be far larger and may have attained a size whereby, of necessity, they are 'balanced' rather than actively 'managed'. In troubled times, a broker fund may go entirely liquid; insurance company managed funds cannot, although an investor could utilise the free switching to transfer into the insurance company's cash fund. The overall market in broker-managed funds stands at 1,000 or more and continues to expand. The main life offices involved are Royal Heritage (the market leader), Target Life, LAS and M&G.

The degree of control exercised by insurance companies

varies from restricting brokers to in-house funds, to giving
free access to any authorised unit trust or insurance fund.
Occasionally, direct equity investment is sanctioned. One
important point to bear in mind is that life company approval
to manage a fund does not necessarily reflect a broker's investment ability; and while your capital may be 'safe' in the sense
that the broker cannot run away with it, it can still be rapidly
diminished by his mistaken investment judgements.

Most brokers charge the same initial fee as would the life
office, typically 5 per cent, but increase the annual charge
by 1 per cent, to between 2 per cent to 2.5 per cent, to
cover their work.

The Right Choice?

Unitised insurance funds are suitable for a limited audience
– essentially, higher rate taxpayers and investors fully liable to
gains tax; particularly if they are looking to convert capital into
income. (See 'Income' section below). Performance wise they
are not as strong as unit trusts, because of the fund's gains tax
liability. Broker funds tend to be a bit of a curate's egg: some
have easily out-performed their life company counterparts;
others, frankly, have been appalling.

Investment Trusts

Investment trusts are different again, being public limited
companies (plc's), which invest in other companies' stocks
and shares. Shares in the investment trust, like any other
quoted on the London Stock Exchange, carry rights to dividend payments and voting at the shareholders' annual general
meeting. The share price will rise and fall in response to
demand, reflecting both the value of the trust's investments
and the future outlook.

Investment trust fans believe that one of their major attractions is that the share price normally stands at a discount to
net asset value – the market worth of the underlying holdings.
If, for example, the discount is 20 per cent (a typical case),
an investor is paying £80 for £100 worth of investments.
The size of the discount will vary with the market's view of
the management team; the higher the esteem, the lower the
discount. The discount in itself, however, is pretty much
immaterial: what matters is how the discount moves – narrows
or widens – during your term of investment. If it narrows,

you'll make an extra 'free' profit when you sell; if it widens, its effect is negative.

Shares in investment trusts are easy to buy, either through a stockbroker, bank or 'share-shop' for a relatively small commission of around £16.50 for £1,000 worth of shares. In some cases, they can be bought commission-free, though including stamp duty and VAT, direct from the management company. Commission is kept to a minimum on the regular savings schemes and so the typical £25 a month minimum is feasible. On lump sums, however, £1,000 is usually considered a realistic minimum.

Several insurance companies offer specialist life insurance and pension funds which invest wholly in investment trusts. Indirect investment is also offered by way of unit trusts and personal equity plans. The investment trust advisory services of stockbrokers such as Alexander Laing & Cruickshank, Touche Remnant and Wood Mackenzie can offer further advice, and the Association of Investment Trust Companies can provide a mass of useful information.

Suitable For You?
Company status allows investment trusts a variety of structure: some gear towards capital growth, others to an increasing income. Split-level trusts offer a combination from a single portfolio: income shareholders take the dividends; growth shares, the bulk of the capital growth.

Like any other unitised investment, they are not suitable for persons who may need their money in a hurry. In the unlikely event of an investment trust going broke, investors simply stand in line for a share of the hand-out following the disposal of assets. Overall, they are suitable for anyone willing to take on some equity risk in the furtherance of higher returns. Investment trusts usually have more broadly spread portfolios than unit trusts.

Income from Unitised Investment
There are two ways of deriving a regular income from unit trusts: investing in one or more high-yielding unit trusts, or by periodic encashment of units.

Many companies offer ready-made income schemes, requiring a minimum investment of between £1,000 and £5,000 spread across several of their trusts, the differing distribution dates allowing for quarterly or sometimes monthly payments. Alternatively, investors may take the DIY route, choosing trusts from a number of management groups, the safety-conscious including both equity and fixed-interest trusts. Income will be tax-free to investors paying basic rate; non-taxpayers may reclaim the tax deducted.

There are only two major drawbacks: the level of income will fluctuate and, at least initially, it may well be low compared to that available from building societies. At current rates, UK Equity Income trusts are yielding between 4 per cent and 6 per cent gross, with gilt income trusts providing around 8 per cent (in some cases up to 11 per cent) compared to between 5 per cent and 7 per cent net of basic rate tax on building society deposits (depending on the amount invested and the period of notice required on withdrawals). However, unlike the return from building society deposits, the income generated by unit trusts should grow with time.

Withdrawal plans offer a way round these problems. Investment is normally by way of accumulation units and having chosen the approximate level of income they require – either a fixed amount or a set percentage, either way usually 5 per cent with a 10 per cent maximum – investors simply cash-in the appropriate number of units at regular intervals. By choosing high-yielding trusts, less of the capital is encashed. Even so, withdrawal plans may only preserve capital in a strong bull market; if the market is static or falling, investors could be eating into their 'seed corn' at an unwittingly fast rate.

For tax purposes the income is considered in two parts: distributions, on which basic rate tax has been paid; and a partial encashment, which could give rise to a gains tax liability, though the amount involved is usually negligible.

Single premium insurance funds are an efficient way for higher rate taxpayers to convert capital into income. Up to 5 per cent of the original investment may be taken tax-free each year for a period of twenty years, higher amounts being liable to higher rate (but not to basic rate) tax.

This '5 per cent for twenty years' allowance can be left to accumulate so if, for example, you have held the investment for ten years and not withdrawn anything from it, you are then allowed to take 10 per cent a year tax-free for the next ten years.

On encashment, there is never any further tax to pay

if you are a basic rate taxpayer; higher rate taxpayers may, however, face an extra charge at that point. People who are eligible for the age allowance against income tax should be especially careful here, as they run the risk of losing some of the age allowance if they withdraw too much income.

Personal Equity Plans

Personal Equity Plans (PEPs) are equity-based investments which, if held for a minimum of one complete calendar year after the year of investment, provide a totally tax-free return. Since they first became available on 1 January 1987, more than eighty companies have entered the fray, offering a variety of schemes ranging from high-risk direct equity ventures, to others taking unit or investment trusts on board. Plans are open to anyone over the age of 18 and resident in the UK for tax purposes, on the basis of one per person per calendar year; married couples are allowed on per partner.

Contributions must be in cash (unless switched out of an existing PEP) and subject to an upper limit of £3,000 a year or £250 a month, plus any additional amounts to take up rights issues or other entitlements. In practice, the minimum investment is £20 a month. All 1988 PEPs will close to new investment on 31 December 1988 and any further contributions must go into a 1989 plan, where the cycle continues.

The original intention of broadening share ownership has never fitted comfortably with the £3,000 maximum investment. That is simply not enough to buy a sufficient number of shares for a properly balanced portfolio. Although the bulk of any investment must be in UK ordinary shares, quoted on either the Stock Exchange or the Unlisted Securities Market (USM), up to £540, or 25 per cent of the total investment (£750 on the full £3,000), may be invested in unit or investment trusts with no stipulation where these are invested. This broader-risk element may be switched between trusts but once transferred into direct equity holdings, cannot be switched back. Once invested, PEPs may only hold cash for up to twenty-eight days and even this is restricted to a maximum of 10 per cent of an investor's total PEP holdings as at the previous December 31.

For the proceeds to be tax-free, plans must be held for at least one complete calendar year, which in practice means that

PEPs started any time during 1988 will mature simultaneously on 1 January 1990. In the jargon, 1989 is the 'holding year' and the period between purchase and maturity, the 'qualifying period'. Switching investments is allowed but since withdrawals will render a plan void, any dividend income is automatically reinvested, without deduction of income tax, towards capital growth.

At maturity, investors may either withdraw the proceeds free of capital gains tax, or leave plans to accumulate further. Holdings may be adjusted without losing the tax benefits. Plans from successive years may be merged, as each reaches maturity, creating one tax-exempt fund.

PEP Charges

A major criticism of PEPs is that the charges tend to be high, so high that in practice, most plan managers allow for the initial charge to be paid on top of the £3,000 upper limit. Although a few schemes impose no initial charge, others charge between 1 per cent and 5 per cent of the investment and yet others levy a flat fee, usually around £25, though it can be as high as £75. Annual charges vary between 1 per cent and 1.5 per cent, sometimes with a fixed minimum. Dealing charges of about 1.65 per cent of the value of shares bought or sold (sometimes included in the annual management charge) and stamp duty at 0.5 per cent on all share purchases, are usually additional items. All PEP charges, with the exception of the 5 per cent initial charge on unit trust holdings, incur VAT.

Although any direct ordinary shareholding entitles the investor to attend that company's annual general meeting, the right is rarely taken up in practice. By law, managers of discretionary funds need only send company reports and accounts to those who ask, although all investors must receive a six-monthly statement explaining purchases and sales. Additional information will normally be charged; often steeply.

Who Has the Most to Gain?

Because of the high charge structure, PEPs offer the most benefit to those who can afford the maximum £3,000 investment in one lump sum. Higher rate taxpayers are also favoured. Assuming the full £3,000 is invested in a scheme yielding 5 per cent a year, basic rate taxpayers stand to gain £34.40 a year in tax savings, a 40 per cent taxpayer saves £49.20p.   Since contributions during the 'investing' year need not be invested in securities until the £3,000 upper limit, or year-end, is reached, the first year's contributions may be held temporarily in a money market deposit account. Again, higher rate taxpayers have the most to gain. Once an investor has PEP funds invested in stocks and shares, all cash must be (re)invested within twenty-eight days.

Peter Fuller

Information and Contacts
Unit Trust Association
Park House, 16 Finsbury Circus London EC2M 7JP; 01-831 0898

Association of Investment Trusts (AITC)
Park House, 16 Finsbury Circus, London EC2M 7JP 01-588 5347

The Securities and Investment Board
3 Royal Exchange Building, London EC3V 3NL 01-283 2474

Alexander Laing & Cruickshank
Piercy House, 7 Copthall Street, London EC2R 7BE 01-588 2800

Touche Remnant
2 Puddle Dock London EC4V 3AT 01-248 1250

Wood Mackenzie & Co
Kintoe House, 74-77 Queen Street, Edinburgh EH2 4NS 031-225 8525

Further Reading

A Guide to Investment Trusts - AITC (address above)

Unit Trust Yearbook - UTA (address above)

Pepguide (latest offerings)
Chase de Vere, 63 Lincolns Inn Fields, London WC2A 3JX
01-404 5766

Money Management
Financial Times Business Information,
Greystoke Place, Fetter Lane, London EC4A 1ND 01-405 6969

Planned Savings and *Savings Market*
Maxwell Corp, 33 Bowling Green Lane, London EC1R
0DA 01-837 1212

6 Planning for School Fees

The Advisability of Planning

School fees can pose a major problem for many parents. It is often difficult to be sure that enough cash will be available at exactly the right time in order to meet this substantial expenditure.

Families with low incomes or several children who will attend private schools at the same time generally find it impossible, or at least very difficult, to meet the fees from earnings alone. Moreover, once a child has started down the private education route, it is usually very undesirable to change course part way through his or her school career.

For all these reasons, it is essential to undertake some planning and the earlier it is started, the easier is the whole process.

The total cost of school fees for a couple of children can be a daunting prospect. Based on average levels of, say, £650 per term for a child from age 7 to 13 and £800 (at present rates) from age 13 to 18, the following table sets out the total commitment to school fees for two children now aged 4 and 7. The table allows for inflation at a rate of 10 per cent per annum and for fees to start from the term beginning in September 1988.

Just consider the amount of gross income which would be needed to fund school fees at these levels if no planning had been undertaken. Assuming the top rate of tax charged is 40 per cent, the gross income needed, for example, in the year starting in September 1997 would be £18,863. What is more, during the children's school careers we shall see at least two General Elections, with a possibility of change in political and economic persuasion. If we look back over the past ten to twelve years, we have seen long periods of inflation at levels of 20 to 25 per cent and top rates of tax at 83 per cent on earnings and 98 per cent on investment income.

The table also ignores the possibility of university education after 'A' levels have been taken at age 18.

School Year Commencing	Child Aged 7 £	Child Aged 4 £	Total £
September 1988	1,950	—	1,950
September 1989	2,145	—	2,145
September 1990	2,360	2,360	4,720
September 1991	2,595	2,595	5,190
September 1992	2,855	2,855	5,710
September 1993	3,865	3,141	7,006
September 1994	4,252	3,455	7,707
September 1995	4,677	3,800	8,477
September 1996	5,155	5,155	10,310
September 1997	5,659	5,659	11,318
September 1998	—	6,225	6,225
September 1999	—	6,848	6,848
September 2000	—	7,532	7,532
	35,513	49,625	85,138

Strategy of Planning

Once the decision has been taken, and the earlier the better, to send your child (or children) to a private school, then perhaps the first step is to try to identify the levels of fees which you are likely to have to pay. This may mean selecting a school well in advance. This could seem unrealistic but it does have certain advantages. Not only will this allow you to consider the probable school fee bill but it may be an advantage to put the child's name down for the school well in advance, to ensure a place when the time comes.

In simple terms, you will be trying to spread the cost of the total school fee bill over as long a period as possible. If there is plenty of time before the fees are needed, you could start a funding programme now which provides for the cash to pay the fees when they are required. The earlier the programme is started, the greater will be the investment advantage. In fact, the most effective planning will be undertaken by the parent who starts to plan even before the child is born!

Where the fees have actually started, then it may be possible to spread the cost by taking a series of loans which are repaid after the education programme has been completed. The second method will be significantly more expensive because interest will have to be paid in the borrowings.

You will then want to take stock of your capital assets and present and future income to help you to pay the bills. You will also want to enlist help from grandparents who may be willing and able to provide cash assistance, and this could bring tax advantages as well.

Help from Grandparents

Where willing grandparents, or other relatives, are available, then they could consider arrangements to provide taxable income in the hands of the children. This will allow the personal tax allowances to be claimed for the children and, as the effective use of Deeds of Covenant has been ended following the last Budget, the only remaining way of achieving this, essentially, is by using Trusts.

This device will not be effective if set up by parents because of anti-avoidance income tax law. Where the parents of minor children make arrangements which result in income being transferred to the child, then the parent will continue to be taxed on that income and the arrangement will not be effective for tax purposes until the child has become 18, or marries.

Deeds of Covenant

Even though this route is no longer available, there will be a number of Deeds of Covenant, which were set up before the Budget, in existence. Those deeds have not been affected by the Budget and will continue to be tax effective. They cannot be extended on the same terms, so envy the far-sighted grandparent who set them up for a period of ten years or more instead of the standard seven-year period.

Trusts

Where the grandparent wishes to gift capital which will provide income for minor children, use can be made of a trust. While there are choices of trust, the most popular one is the Accumulation and Maintenance Trust.

This can be a most flexible instrument which allows income to be accumulated or distributed amongst the grandchildren. Where income is accumulated, then tax is charged to the trustees at the rate of 35 per cent. Where income is distributed, then it is regarded as the child's income so that it is effectively tax-free up to the level of the Single Personal Allowance for each child.

Where assets are gifted to the trustees, the effects of

capital taxation on gifts should be considered. The two taxes concerned are Capital Gains Tax and Inheritance Tax, and neither should present a problem. Capital Gains Tax can be postponed until the sale of the assets by the trustees, if both the grandparent and the trustees elect to do so. Inheritance Tax will not be payable if the grandparents survive for seven years after the gift has been made.

Whilst any asset can be gifted to the trust, an interesting choice could be shares in a private family company. The gifts to the trust by the grandparent can be beneficial also for Inheritance Tax purposes.

Once the shares are owned by the trustees, income can be created by payment of dividends from the family company. Other shareholders can waive their dividend entitlement without adverse tax consequences, so that the trustees are the only shareholders who actually retain their dividends. In the present climate, where National Insurance Contributions are payable by the employer at 10.45 per cent on salary, there is a tendency to pay remuneration by the dividend route.

On the other hand, if other shareholders do waive their dividends, there is just the possibility that the Revenue could argue that a shareholding parent is responsible for indirectly creating funds for the trust by the dividend waiver mechanism. This argument is a little far-fetched although, following the success achieved by the Revenue with the Courts on associated operations creating tax advantage, it should not be wholly discounted.

The income from the trust can then be distributed to the parent who can use it to meet school fees for the child.

Fees from Capital

Where capital is to be used from the parents' resources, then there are a number of investments which could be considered. Some typical vehicles are Educational trusts, Personal Equity Plans, National Savings Certificates, Investment Bonds, British Government Securities, Annuities and Business Expansion Schemes. Most of these will have the effect of consuming the original capital plus any investment advantage which is achieved. Clearly it pays to look at tax efficient investments, and flexibility is absolutely essential in case there is a change of plan.

Educational Trusts

Educational Trusts are available from several sources including Save & Prosper, Royal Life, Equitable Life and School Fees Insurance Agency. As the parent or grandparent, you can make a lump-sum investment with an educational trust which will guarantee payments tailored to meet fees at pre-selected times. The payments can be level or increasing and the guarantees are usually met through the purchase of an annuity.

The investment returns are better for higher rate taxpayers because the proceeds are not subject to income tax.

The main disadvantage of this approach is its inflexibility. If the child is not able to attend private school, then you could suffer some loss on your investment.

Personal Equity Plans

The Personal Equity Plan is the latest scheme introduced by the present Government to encourage investment in equity markets. Once capital up to a maximum of £3,000 per person has remained within a qualifying scheme for a complete calendar year, then the income and capital gains are free of tax from the original date of investment. This would be of greater advantage to higher rate taxpayers and individuals who are using up the whole of their exempt gains band (presently £5,000) for capital gains tax purposes each year.

The real disadvantage is the risk undertaken by investing in equities when funds will be needed at a particular time as part of a school fees plan. This type of plan would have succeeded very well if it had been available three to four years ago when equity markets were in a bull phase, but an investment made just before 'Black Monday' in October 1987 could look fairly bleak despite its tax attractions.

National Savings Certificates

National Savings Certificates can provide a guaranteed and tax-free income return, which is particularly attractive when received by higher rate taxpayers. Once the certificate has been held for a period of five years, the extension rate of interest will be received so that the certificates provide a safe home to meet fees in the medium term.

Investment Bonds and Unit Trusts
Both these investment vehicles can provide varying risk pro-
files, as you can choose to invest in equities, property, fixed
interest etc. A comparison of the tax treatment between the
two could be an important determining factor when choosing one or other of them. The high rate taxpayer might
lean towards the investment bond, although the advantage
of postponement of higher rate tax on withdrawals could be
more than offset at the final surrender of the bond to pay fees.
The bond would be likely to be more attractive if withdrawals
of not more than 5 per cent a year are taken to pay the fees,
as these are free of tax.

British Government Securities
This is a secure, if unexciting, method of guaranteeing payment. A lump sum of capital can be invested in specific dated
stocks, thus ensuring that known amounts of capital will be
available at specific dates in the future for payment of fees.

The income tax position of the parent can determine
whether investment is made into high or low interest rate
securities. A basic rate taxpayer might prefer a high interest
rate with the intention of investing the income as it arises. A
high rate taxpayer might prefer tax-free capital gains in order
to keep taxable income to a minimum.

The prices of gilts are, of course, sensitive to changes in
interest rates so that an investment programme, once started,
should not be disturbed if the guarantee of payment of school
fees is important.

Annuities
The range of annuities - ie immediate, deferred, temporary
and capital protected - can be used either singly, or in combination, to provide an attractive method of investment for
school fee payments. An annuity can provide guarantees and is
widely used by educational trusts with even greater advantage
because of the beneficial tax treatment.

However, annuity rates are sensitive to interest rates.
The problem is that the rate at the time of purchase remains
constant throughout the term of the annuity. If, therefore,
the yield is lower at the time of purchase, then the contract
will be prejudiced throughout its life.

Business Expansion Schemes

This style of investment is likely to carry the highest risk, although the tax advantages can be significant to a high rate taxpayer. The minimum term of the investment must be five years if the full tax advantages are to be achieved. This could, therefore, be an ideal investment for the medium-term school fees plan.

Disadvantages of this scheme are the risk exposure, the lack of control over the investment, the fact that the investment is locked up for five years and the lack of a ready market for the shares even when the five-year period has been completed. Some of these can be reduced by careful selection of the issuing institution or by investing in a basket of shares.

The real advantage is the beneficial tax treatment on investments of up to £40,000 per annum. A top rate taxpayer (40 per cent) will obtain £10,000 of investment at a cost of only £6,000, so the £4,000 tax subsidy could be a persuasive argument to accept the disadvantages.

After the Budget changes in Business Expansion Schemes we shall have to wait and see the effects on the numbers and types of companies who will be looking for finance through this route. This may cut down the choices of investing in this medium.

Fees from Income and Savings

If you have done little or no planning, then current income will mostly be used to meet fees as they arise. Some help may be available from grandparents using trusts and the tax saving could give considerable help. If there is surplus income available, then it can be used to help in funding future fees. The greatest scope for savings from income will mostly arise before the child has started school, or in the earlier stages when fees are lower.

Since the Chancellor has reduced the top rate of tax from 1988/89 from 60 per cent to 40 per cent, higher earners will find that the extra net amount they receive will ease the burden of funding direct from income. A change of fiscal policy could, however, reverse this new trend.

This income can be capitalised and used in a lump-sum funding scheme or, if there is sufficient time, it can be used to pay the premium for a cluster of endowment policies in which the underlying investment is either unit-linked or with-profits. As a known figure will be required to meet the fees, many people prefer the less volatile with-profits route.

Endowment Policies

This method works best when fees are payable in ten years or more. Usually, there is not so much time available and, at a pinch, loans can be taken against the policies and repaid at the maturity of the first policy in the cluster after ten years. After the first policy has matured, the monthly premiums will be reduced so that there is a tapering down effect in the cost.

For example, fees are required at the level of £1,000 per term starting in January 1995, and the parent is allowing for inflation at 10 per cent per annum and basing calculations on the school year starting in September. There is also an allowance for a significant increase from September 1997 when the child has become 11 years old. The fees required would look like this:

Year Commencing September	Fees Required £
1994	2,000
1995	3,330
1996	3,663
1997	5,322
1998	5,853
1999	6,441
2000	7,083
2001	7,791
2002	8,571
2003	9,429
	59,483

In order to produce this level of fees, a major with-profits life company has quoted for a cluster of seven policies, maturing from years ten to sixteen, to provide the fees. From September 1994 the fees would be provided by loans and the accumulated total of loans and interest would be repaid when the first policy matured after year ten. After that, the premiums will reduce and the quotation would look like this:

In the example the total payment to the insurance company

Year	Cumulative Loans & Interest £	Term of Policy (years)	Projected Maturity Value £	Total Monthly Premium £	Total Annual Contribution £
1988-93					2821*
1994	2000			235.12	2821
1995	5892			235.12	2821
1996	10376			235.12	2821
1997	17156	10	17156	235.12	2821
1998		11	5853	146.22	1755
1999		12	6441	119.43	1433
2000		13	7083	93.85	1126
2001		14	7791	69.26	831
2002		15	8571	45.53	546
2003		16	9429	22.44	269

*Annual payments of £2,821 in each of the years 1988 to 1993.

will have been £34,174 in order to provide fees of £59,483. Perhaps more importantly, the cost will have been spread over sixteen years to fund fees arising over a period of ten years.

In the quotation, the life company has allowed for the policy to be taken out on the joint lives of the parents, where the father is 36 and the mother is 35. The monthly premium at the start of the arrangement would be £235.12. The interest on loans would be charged at 13.5 per cent a year and the projected maturity values have been calculated in accordance with the Industry Code of Practice.

Use of Loan Plans
If you have undertaken no planning to meet the school fees, and fees cannot be funded from current income, then a loan plan is likely to be the only solution. Most loan plans lend funds over a long-term period and look for security such as a second mortgage.

The method of repaying the loan is usually an insurance policy, although some borrowers will accept capital from the commutation of a pension plan. This method is the most expensive way of funding school fees, but has to be adopted if you have no alternative.

Raymond Godfrey

7 Why Pensions?

A pension is the income you will receive when you retire, when your earnings stop. However, there will only be any money for you after retirement if it has been arranged long beforehand. 'Pension planning' is putting money aside during your working lifetime. Since retirement is many years away, that money will be put to work in the meantime, and the investment returns will add to your benefits when you come to retire. A pension plan is a long-term investment.

But if pensions are a simple process, pension schemes are anything but simple. First, there are three separate legs to your pension stool: the State, your employer and your own personal retirement savings. Part of the State leg is optional. Next, there are various different ways in which both you and your employer can save for retirement. Finally, the Government gives many valuable tax incentives to encourage retirement provision, but these are governed by a myriad of rules and regulations. The simple investment process has become a maze of options. And it can be difficult to plan a route through the maze when you are still young enough for pension provision to be affordable. The trouble is that pensions only start to get attractive when you are pretty close to them. By then the cost of anything worthwhile has become prohibitive.

We cannot blame all the obscurity on the legislators, the insurance companies and the pension consultants. The fact is that most people take no interest in pensions until they get within sight of them. But there has been a flood of recent legislation affecting pension schemes, which means more people have started to give pensions the attention they deserve. Perhaps only now can we start to see the pensions wood for the pension scheme trees.

State Pensions
The first pension leg is the State. Everyone who retires with a full National Insurance contribution record will get the basic state pension when they retire, at 65 for males

or 60 for females. At present the Basic State Pension is
£39.50 per week for a single person and £63.25 per week for
a married couple.

In April 1978 a second state pension scheme started.
Introduced by Barbara Castle, it was to provide a second
state pension to all employed people. This State Earnings
Related Pension Scheme, or SERPS as it has become known,
would give all employees an additional pension of up to one
quarter of their average earnings. And this pension would be
protected against inflation both during the working career and
after retirement.

Right from the start employers who operated 'good'
company schemes could opt out of SERPS, and indeed
were encouraged to do so by lower rates of employer and
employee National Insurance contributions. This was called
'contracting out' and most employees in company schemes
were contracted out.

Pay-As-You-Go Pensions

Basic State Pensions, and SERPS, are run on a 'Pay-as-
you-go' basis. This means that no separate fund of money
is put aside, but instead the Government meets each year's
pensions out of that year's take on National Insurance contributions. Because the Government always has the option
of raising taxes to meet the pension spend as the number of
pensioners increases, this is seen as reasonable. Whether or
not it is prudent is another matter. It certainly would not
work for the other two pension legs, namely the employer's pension promise and your own provision. These two
pensions can only be as secure as the investments made
to support them. These pensions will be 'funded', that is
backed up by savings, by means of a trust fund established
by your employer, or by the resources of an insurance company.

Company Pension Schemes

About 11 million employees already belong to company
pension schemes. These schemes come in all shapes and
sizes. There are good schemes and not-so-good schemes.
There are also two distinct types: Final Salary schemes and
Money Purchase schemes.

Final Salary Schemes

Final Salary schemes, as the name suggests, promise members a pension related to the level of their earnings at or near retirement. A typical good scheme would promise a pension of one-sixtieth of your average earnings in the last three years of employment for every year you have been a member. For example, someone completing thirty years' service would get an annual income of 30/60ths, or one-half of his final average salary. In practice, many Final Salary schemes will not look exactly like this but the principle will be the same.

The actual size of the pension which will eventually be paid from a Final Salary scheme cannot be determined in advance. Your final salary itself will not be known until you retire. However members can have confidence that the pension will be worthwhile, whatever happens to such things as inflation, because the prospective pension will increase every time the salary increases. A Final Salary scheme can be said to be inflation-proof, and this is why they have been regarded as the best type of pension scheme to have.

For the employer, a Final Salary pension scheme carries an uncertainty on the long-term cost. Even if employees themselves contribute (5 per cent would be a typical employee contribution rate), the employer will have to meet the balance of the cost whatever that might be. Several years of salary inflation could increase his contribution significantly. There have also been times when very good investment returns have allowed an employer to cut back on his contributions. Because of this uncertainty of long-term costs, Final Salary pension schemes have been more common in larger companies.

There is another important point about Final Salary pension schemes. The employer will invariably pay an 'average' rate of contribution to the scheme. This average contribution hides the fact that the actual cost of a pension varies according to age. The cost for an employee in his fifties is considerably greater than the cost for someone in their twenties. The average contribution rate is paid as a convenience. This means that you cannot judge the value of a scheme just by looking at the employer's contribution rate. A company with a large number of young employees may have a better scheme than another employer, even though it is costing him less. And vice versa. There are often other, historical reasons why schemes with very similar benefits might be costing two employers very different amounts. It is not the cost to the employer, but the benefits his scheme promises to pay, which is important.

Money Purchase Schemes

Money Purchase schemes are much simpler than Final Salary schemes. The employer pays a fixed contribution for each member, and that contribution is earmarked for the member in an individual pot right from the start. The investment income is added to each pot every year, so it is always easy to see how much money is held for each member. In this respect a Money Purchase scheme works very like a building society account, although the investments themselves will usually be different.

The advantage of a Money Purchase scheme for the employee is its simplicity. It is easier to see the invest-ment process, and to put a value on his membership. Unlike the Final Salary scheme, there is no cross-subsidy between members of different ages and sex. An employer likes the fixed contributions, relaxed that inflation will not cause increases in his future costs. But that is also a serious weakness of Money Purchase. The resulting benefits are hostage to inflation and investment returns. Anyone retiring from a Money Purchase scheme on 17 October 1987 would have discovered his benefits had reduced by some 20 per cent overnight. Not a happy end to a long pension scheme membership. Of course it is possible to create reserves to help meet this problem, by smoothing out investment returns, but this would only be a par-tial solution.

Some modern pension schemes now combine the features of both Final Salary and Money Purchase arrangements. For example, a scheme might offer salary-related pensions, but underpin this with a guaranteed benefit equal in value to a certain level of contributions with interest. These are called 'hybrid' schemes.

Until 1988 the only company pension schemes that could 'contract out' of SERPS were Final Salary schemes, but this condition has now been dropped. The second type of scheme, Money Purchase, can also now be used for contracting out. This is one of the new incentives for smaller companies to operate 'contracted-out' pension schemes.

The New Legislation

The aim of much of the recent legislation is to encourage more employers and individuals to make their own secure pension investments, and to rely less on the State. An ageing population means that the rising cost of SERPS would prove a severe embarrassment to the Government after the turn of the century. So the benefits of SERPS have been cut back in several ways. Anyone retiring after the year 2000 will receive at most 20 per cent rather than 25 per cent of average earnings. Furthermore, the average is a poorer one since it is taken over the full working career, not just the best twenty years. These reductions in SERPS will not apply to anyone retiring before the year 2000.

At the same time, new incentives have been given to employers to encourage them both to establish new company schemes and to contract out of SERPS. The Government has also introduced new Personal Pensions to give all employees, whether they are in a company scheme or not, the option of making their own arrangements. This new flexibility sounds attractive, and so it might be except that, because pensions have become so complicated, not many employees will have all the information they will need to make a good choice.

The Decision for Pension Scheme Members

There is no decision to make about the Basic State Pension since everyone will continue to be entitled to that as at present.

An employee in a company scheme has several options. First, he can do nothing and remain a member of the company scheme as before. But he does not have to, because since 6 April 1988 employees have had the right to leave an employer's scheme. If he leaves and does not start a personal pension he will get the basic state pension and SERPS (but he would keep any past pensions he already has).

Leaving a company scheme just to rely on SERPS is not likely to be very attractive, and it is certainly not what the Government had in mind when they introduced these reforms. Not only are his prospective pension benefits likely to be worse, but strangely his take-home pay could reduce! This could happen if his company pension scheme was contracted out, and his National Insurance contribution rebate was bigger than the contributions he had to pay into the scheme. He would then get less for more - not a sensible decision! In checking this point, remember that pension scheme contributions are tax-deductible whereas National Insurance contributions are not.

For example, the National Insurance rebate from April 1988 for an employee whose scheme was contracted out will be 2 per cent. A basic rate taxpayer paying less than 2.67 per cent of the same salary band to the company scheme would find his costs increase if he leaves the scheme.

Swapping the Company Scheme for A Personal Pension

To leave the company scheme and start a personal pension is a different matter, and the decision is not so straightforward. In this case the member will usually have to compare pension benefits from the employer's scheme with a personal pension scheme. And this will be like comparing chalk with cheese if the scheme is Final Salary, since the personal pension will always be Money Purchase (a final salary personal pension is not possible since there is no employer to pick up the balance of cost).

The comparison would be difficult even if you had a good view of future investment returns, future inflation and salary rises, and indeed knew whether you would stay in one scheme until retirement, or whether you might die or retire early in ill health. Since there is no way you can know the answers to all (and possibly any) of these questions, the alternative is to compare the actual costs of the two routes rather than their possible future benefits.

A very important point to bear in mind is that the employer need not contribute to the personal pension even if he would otherwise make large contributions to the company scheme for that member. If this is the case, the personal pension is going to start with a significant disadvantage. Not only that, the contributions you would make to a personal pension policy would include hidden expenses, which would reduce the amount actually being invested for you. It is likely that any expenses in the company's scheme will be met by the employer himself.

You must also determine what extra benefits your company scheme might provide that the personal pension could not; and take into account how you feel your future career might develop and your own personal preferences. Never turn down the option of staying in or joining your company's scheme

without considering the benefits other than pension which
it gives. Most schemes give valuable life assurance benefits,
and lump-sum retirement benefits, which would add to the
cost of your personal pension. And the personal pension could
probably not match the ill-health retirement benefits of your
company scheme. Your company scheme might also have
benefits which it doesn't advertise but which would be very
difficult to replace. Many good schemes give their pensioners
regular increases on an *ex gratia* basis - benefits not guaranteed
but which they hope to continue indefinitely.

Changing Jobs

There was a time when employees would forfeit their
company pension benefits if they changed jobs. But since 6
April 1988, anyone who has been in a pension scheme at least
two years must be allowed to keep his benefits. The scheme
must pay you the pension you have earned when you retire.
This pension will have to be increased by that scheme, but
it will not usually be fully inflation-proofed (although local
government schemes and civil service schemes are a notable
exception: benefits left behind in these schemes will be fully
protected against inflation).

But the member who leaves a scheme after at least two
years' membership has two other options. He may choose
to take a 'transfer value' to his next employer's scheme. The
transfer value is the sum of money equal in value to his pension rights in the job he is leaving. If he chooses this option
the new employer will give him some extra benefits in the
new scheme. Secondly, the leaving member can ask for this
transfer to be used to buy a 'one-off' pension policy from an
insurance company chosen by the individual himself. This
is called a Section 32 policy after the section of the Act
which permits it.

These three options on leaving a scheme are for the
member to choose, not his employer. It is not possible
to give categorical advice here, and you would need expert
independent advice. However, leaving benefits behind in a
fully inflation-protected scheme is usually a good option. If
your new employer operates a good scheme it is most likely
that he will offer 'good' extra benefits in return for the
transfer value. A section 32 policy might suit best someone
whose next employer does not operate a scheme, but such a

person should also consider a transfer to a new-style personal pension to which he can also make future contributions.

So the likelihood of future job changes is not itself a good reason to desert a company pension scheme and start a personal pension.

Additional Voluntary Contributions

There is a suitable alternative to personal pensions for anyone who is in a company scheme. Instead of giving up the benefits of the company scheme, you can add to them by paying Additional Voluntary Contributions, known as AVCs. These savings are tax-deductible, and like all approved pension arrangements, roll up free of tax. All pension schemes must make an AVC scheme available to their members from April 1988. Furthermore, since October 1987, 'free-standing' AVCs have been available. This means members may choose to join the employer's suggested AVC scheme, or choose their own personal AVC from an insurance company, building society or bank of their choice.

The tax advantages mean there is no better way of making long-term saving. You must realise, however, that these particular savings may not be used for holidays, new cars, house improvements etc – at least not until you have retired and started to draw benefits.

Your AVCs, together with any contributions that you pay to your employer's scheme, must not exceed 15 per cent of your taxable earnings. However you may use AVCs for occasional savings. For example, if you received an unexpected bonus, on which you will have to pay income tax, you could put some or all of that bonus into an AVC and your tax will then be reduced. Furthermore you have made no commitment for the future. Next year's bonus can be used for a cruise if you prefer.

On paying AVCs, you will have to watch out for Inland Revenue limits. These are described later, and are the maximum benefits you are allowed to take from an approved scheme, including the benefits from AVCs. There is a danger that if you are in a good company scheme, and you pay large AVCs, and these earn a good investment yield, then you could lose some of your total entitlement. Whilst this is unlikely (the Revenue limits are higher than you might imagine), you should take advice from

your pension fund manager or the AVC provider before
making AVCs.

AVCs For Pension Not Cash

Any AVC arrangement started after 8 April 1987 can only
be used to supplement your pension benefits. AVCs started
before then can be used to add to your lump-sum retirement
benefit (subject to Inland Revenue limits described later).
However, it is likely that you will be able to take a larger lump
sum from your employer's scheme itself if you are using AVCs
to boost your pension. You will have to check the details for
your particular scheme with your pension manager.

If your company scheme is not 'contracted out' of SERPS,
and the advantages of doing so appeal to you (these are mentioned later), you can use a free-standing AVC to contract out,
which means that in addition to your own contributions the
AVC would receive the contracting-out rebate of National
Insurance contributions. These are 5.8 per cent of your
earnings between £2,132 and £15,860 per annum, split as to
2 per cent from your own National Insurance contributions
and 3.8 per cent from your employer's. In addition there is a
special 2 per cent of these earnings to be given as a bonus by
the DHSS for employees contracting out for the first time.
This bonus will only run from April 1987 until April 1993.

No Company Scheme

Employees who work for a company which does not have
a company scheme, and which does not yet intend to start
one in spite of the new incentives, have only the option of
personal pension policies. They could choose to do nothing,
but that would be to ignore their need for extra income in
retirement. They would also be allowing some valuable tax
advantages to go by default. For someone on average national
earnings, about £180 per week or £9,400 per annum, the basic
state pension and SERPS would total only about 50 per cent
of earnings, or only around 40 per cent for a single person.
And these state pensions will increase in future in line with
rising prices not rising earnings, so the percentages could be
much less by the time you retire in maybe twenty, thirty or
forty years from now. Relying only on the State for pension
provision is not to be recommended.

If you are going to make savings during your working life,

then it would be foolish not to take a personal pension to take advantage of the tax incentives. All contributions paid by an employee to a personal pension policy are deductible against income tax. For a basic taxpayer (paying 25 per cent) this means that every £10 put aside out of taxed income is matched by £3.33 from the taxman. And for someone paying tax at 40 per cent, his £10 would be matched by £6.66. Furthermore, all these contributions are invested tax-free, which should make a considerable difference: private savings in a building society would roll up at a net rate of interest of, say, 6.5 per cent, while the personal pension savings would earn gross interest of, say, 9 per cent. Over twenty-five years, this small discrepancy in yields becomes very significant.

Rate of interest	6.5% pa	9% pa	
Value of £100 per annum after 25 years	£5,889	£8,470	+44%

Not only will your investments perform better inside a tax-free personal pension policy, but the policy can also include valuable life assurance benefits.

So, if you do not have the option of joining a company pension scheme, a personal pension will be an excellent investment. Two decisions remain. Should you 'contract out' of SERPS, and where should you look for the best personal pension?

Contracting Out – Or Not

First, contracting out. This is your decision. If you do not, you will be entitled to the normal SERPS benefit. If you do, you will forgo any SERPS benefits from then on (but you would keep your entitlement to any SERPS you already have in respect of your membership of SERPS since 1978). The advantage of contracting out is that some of your and your employer's National Insurance contributions will be paid into your own personal pension policy instead of to the Government. The question is, therefore, are these contributions worth more than the SERPS benefits you would be giving up?

The cost of a pension depends very much on age. The closer you are to your retirement age then the more expensive a pension will be. For example, to buy an annuity of £1,000 a year for a 65-year-old man might be £10,000. This cost could be met by five annual payments from age 60 of £1,700 (these payments with interest added would accumulate to £10,000). But if you started saving at the age of 40, the cost would be just £136 a year.

The saving in National Insurance contributions is the same for all employees, regardless of age. The reduction has been calculated by the Government actuary as an average. So, generally speaking, contracting out will be good value for younger employees, whilst staying in SERPS will be better value for those nearer retirement.

Men under 45 and women under 40 in 1988 will probably be better off with a personal pension that is contracted out of SERPS. Those with less than ten years to go before state pension age will almost certainly find that staying in SERPS is the best value for money: they can still take out a personal pension to add to the SERPS benefits, though they won't, of course, get the National Insurance rebates to sweeten the pill.

In between is a 'grey area' where it is impossible to state with absolute certainty whether people would be better off contracting out or staying put in SERPS. It depends on how well investments perform, and what inflation is going to be like between now and your retirement – and it also depends on how good a deal the personal pension provides in terms of its charges and expenses.

It is a good idea to get independent advice on this, if you can (there is a list of sources for advice at the end of this chapter); but you should be clear that there is no 'right' answer here - it depends on too many imponderables. Staying in SERPS means taking less risk; contracting out means you *might* do better, if the investment wind is set fair.

The decision is easier for the self-employed: they have never been included in SERPS and so do not have a choice to make. Unless they take out their own personal pension, they will only have the basic state pension to look forward to.

There are other points to take into account. Your personal pension would be much more flexible than SERPS. You will have the option to vary contributions when you can afford to put aside a little more. You can also include benefits not offered by SERPS such as lump-sum retirement benefits, and better spouse's benefits. Of course, your personal pension policy will move with you whenever you change jobs.

Which Personal Pension?

Choosing the right personal pension will not be so easy. You will be bombarded with quotations from the insurance companies, and for the first time the banks, building societies and unit trust organisations who can now enter this market. All this zealous promotion will have a cost – and this cost and any commissions payable to the agent will be hidden in the contributions you pay. This makes comparisons difficult. The future projections of possible (but not guaranteed) benefits gives plenty of scope for the provider's imagination!

Some employers who are not able to offer their own company pension scheme may be able to arrange special group terms for personal pensions from one particular company. It should be able to provide better terms and in particular lower sales expenses and savings in administration costs. The employer cannot compel an employee to join such a group arrangement, but it would be a good starting point for the employee. It is possible that an employer could offer a special extra incentive, such as a contribution from him over and above the contracted-out rebate.

Pension Scheme Death Benefits

There is another tax advantage of pension arrangements which should not be overlooked. Lump-sum death benefits from company schemes are normally free of inheritance tax. These benefits are usually paid 'at the discretion of the trustees', and because the trustees decide to whom the benefits are paid they are not regarded as part of the deceased member's estate. Whilst the trustees must make the decision (otherwise this tax advantage would be lost), members can indicate their wishes in a letter to the trustees. Since the benefits are free of inheritance tax, it is a good opportunity to nominate your children rather than your spouse. Any personal assets you leave to your spouse will be free of inheritance tax anyway, whereas personal assets you leave to your children are taxable.

Inland Revenue Limits

The tax advantages of pension funds are considerable. Both the employee and employer contributions are tax-deductible: the investments roll up free of both income and capital gains tax; and the lump-sum benefits paid at retirement or on death are tax-free. But in case we should enjoy too much of a good thing, the Inland Revenue imposes certain indirect limits on pension benefits.

The Inland Revenue limits the total benefits you may take from approved retirement arrangements (and if it is not Revenue-approved you do not get the tax advantages). The limits are quite detailed, and are inclusive of benefits from other schemes and previous employments. There are also important exceptions, but the major points are described below.

These limits apply to most company schemes and AVCs. They do *not* apply to personal pensions and to certain Money Purchase company schemes which are limited instead to contributions of 17.5 per cent of earnings.

These Inland Revenue limits are defined in terms of 'final salary'. Final Salary means the best year's basic salary in the five years before retirement, together with the average over three years of any fluctuating earnings. Alternatively, you may use the average of any three consecutive years' gross earnings in the thirteen years before retirement. In either case, Final Salary is limited to £150,000 (except for people still in a scheme which was not subject to this limit when it was introduced on 17 March 1987). Individual years' earnings may be adjusted to allow for increase in the Index of Retail Prices since the end of the year in which the salary was drawn. Your scheme will probably have a different definition of Final Salary. It is the Revenue definition given here which counts in deciding whether you are exceeding the Revenue limits or not.

Inland Revenue limits also depend on 'service'. This means the length of time you have been employed by the company which established the scheme, and is not restricted just to the period you have been a member of the pension scheme concerned.

The maximum pension at normal pension age is two-thirds of Final Salary, provided you have twenty years' of service. Those with less service are restricted to a pension of one-thirtieth of Final Salary for each year of service. Lower limits apply for retirement before normal pension age (unless the retirement is for serious ill health).

The maximum lump sum (tax-free) which you may take on retirement is 3/80th of Final Salary for each year of service. However, provided you are entitled to a pension greater than

1/60th for each year of service, you may have a larger lump sum. The absolute maximum, for those on maximum pension and provided twenty years' service has been completed, is one-and-a-half times Final Salary.

Pension Mortgages

Pension mortgages are now often seen as an alternative to repayment or endowment mortgages. The attraction is that a lender will grant an interest-only mortgage because the capital will be repaid from your retirement lump sum. And this lump sum can be built up with tax deductible contributions to a pension scheme, a pre-8 April 1987 AVC policy or a personal pension policy. So there is more tax relief available on a pensions mortgage.

The lender has never been able to take a legal charge on the pension benefit since it is an Inland Revenue condition that pension benefits cannot be assigned or mortgaged. Nevertheless, the lender can take comfort from the existence of the retirement benefits, and of course has a legal charge on the house itself.

Since the advantage is tax, a pension mortgage is more likely to appeal to the higher rate taxpayer. He is probably going to be older too. A 25-year-old might pay a little less per month on a pension mortgage, but if he added up all the interest he will pay until he retires in forty years' time he would probably prefer the ordinary repayment mortgage or an endowment mortgage.

The snag of a pension mortgage is that it might lead to a serious reduction in the standard of living after retirement, since the lump sum has gone to repay the loan. Again the older, higher rate taxpayer is more likely to have other investments (share schemes, stock options etc) which make this less of a problem for him.

Recently, the Revenue have indicated that they do not approve of pension policies being 'marketed' as part of a mortgage package. It is possible that less will be heard of pension mortgages in future.

Retirement Ages

Most pension schemes provide for men to retire at 65 and women at 60. These are the retirement ages under the state scheme. There is a trend towards lower retirement ages for

men, but this will be a slow process because of the high cost
involved. There is also a trend to earlier retirement generally,
and people may retire from age 50 under a personal pension
policy. Early retirement from 50 is also permitted in most pension schemes, although lower Inland Revenue benefit limits
are imposed for retirement below 60 (except on the grounds
of serious ill health, in which case immediate retirement on
full benefits at any age is permitted).

However, since 7 November 1987 employers cannot force
men and women to retire from work at different ages even if
there are different pension ages in the scheme. In other words,
a woman may choose to stay in service until 65 if men can,
and notwithstanding any entitlement she may have to retire
on full pension at 60.

Finally

You should now appreciate how complicated pension arrangements can be, and the difficult choices that may be
facing you. The first step for anyone who is already in
a company pension scheme is the pensions department of
your own company, to find out precisely what benefits you
are getting, and at what cost to yourself.

However, it is not easy to get impartial advice on whether
you should move to a personal pension. Financial advisers
have a vested interest in persuading you to move, so they
can earn a commission on your personal pension.

Still, here are a few rules of thumb to help you decide:

1. If you are in a good Final Salary company scheme,
there is no contest. Stay where you are. A 'good' scheme
is hard to define, but if it gives a pension of at least 1/80th
of Final Salary per year of service and costs you nothing, or
gives you a pension of 1/60th, it can be called 'good'.

2. If you are in a Money Purchase company scheme and
your employer refuses point blank to make any contribution to
a personal pension on your behalf, then again there is likely to
be no contest. Stay with the scheme, and if you want to make
extra retirement savings use AVCs or free-standing AVCs.

3. If you are an employee without a company pension
scheme, you will be a member of SERPS. You can:
i) do nothing and stay in SERPS;
ii) take a personal pension and contract out of SERPS; or
iii) take a personal pension and stay in SERPS as well.

Option iii) is undoubtedly the best if you are within ten years of retirement, though it will cost more than option i). If you are younger, then ii) is the best choice for you.

4. If you are self-employed, the choice is easy. If you do not start a personal pension you will only get the basic state pension when you retire. Get saving with a personal pension.

The really knotty problems come if you don't exactly fit any of these – what to do if your company scheme is only middling, or if you think you will be changing jobs frequently. More difficult still is that grey area when contracting out is marginal. If you are in your fifties and in a contracted-out Money Purchase scheme giving benefits only slightly better than SERPS, you will have to consider leaving that scheme and rejoining SERPS to get the benefit of a Final Salary scheme rather than be hostage to investment returns.

The one basic principle to remember is that the only way of enjoying a good income in retirement is to make sure it is saved up for during your working life – it is too late after that – and that doing it by means of some type of pension scheme is far and away the most tax efficient method.

Adrian Waddingham

Information and Contacts
The Company Pensions Information Centre
7 Old Park Lane
London
W1Y 3LJ
01-493 4757

An independent publisher of pensions booklets including: *What are Personal Pensions? How a pension fund works, How changing jobs affects your pension* (available free of charge)

The Occupational Pensions Advisory Service
Room 327
Aviation House
129 Kingsway
London WC2B 6NN
01-405 6922

A charity offering advice and assistance on all pension scheme matters to members of the public.

The Association of Consulting Actuaries
c/o Watson House
London Road
Reigate
Surrey RH2 9PQ

Consulting actuaries will give independent advice on all aspects of pension schemes. The Association will provide a list of members.

The Society of Pension Consultants
Ludgate House
Ludgate Circus
London EC4A 2AB

The representative association of firms engaged in pensions consultancy.

8 Insurance:
You and Yours

Insurance has to be the bedrock of all financial planning, yet for all its importance, most people find the topic singularly uninteresting. The salesman's motto – insurance is never bought, it's always sold – is not without foundation. But this is not quite fair: there comes a point when the insurance policy suddenly makes fascinating reading – after the event, when it's too late to change.

This chapter should help you get it right before the event.

Life Assurance
The most valuable thing you have to insure, naturally, is you – or to be more prosaic about it, your earning power. Life assurance policies come in many shapes and forms, but before making any decision on this, you should form an estimate of the sort of sum that would be required, should you suddenly be removed from the scene. Filling in your own questionnaire along the lines of the one shown should help.

The need for life assurance is at its greatest if you have one or more people financially dependent on you; typically, if you are the sole wage earner with a young family. But there are other situations where it may be equally pertinent: elderly parents may be dependent on your support, or you may be supplying essential (if unpaid) services which would cost money to replace – colloquially known as 'just a housewife'. Or you may simply have large debts, and the responsibility of paying them may be your only bequest to your heirs.

Life assurance policies may be divided into two broad types: 'protection' policies, which only pay out on your death, and policies which provide a mixture of protection and savings, where you will be able to get your hands on at any rate some of your money while you're still alive. The size of the premiums you pay will depend partly on

How Much Life Cover Do You Need?

You will probably need two types of policy: one to pay out a lump sum, to take care of your debts (eg the mortgage) and one to pay out on income – particularly if you have young children – so that your widow need not to go back to work. If you're both working (and both intend to continue working) your needs are probably less. Work out your particular needs from the following questionnaire:

1. Lump sum requirement
a) What debts do you have?
for example:

Mortgage	£	....
Hire purchase	£	....
Bank overdraft	£	....
Personal loans	£	....
Other	£	....
Sub total(1)	£	....

b) What capital expenditure would be required if you died?
for example:

Replacement of company car	£	....
Funeral expenses	£	....
Other	£	....
Sub total(2)	£	....

Total required for term assurance   £ ....
less any already provided for in company pension scheme   £ ....

Grand Total   £...............

2. Income requirement
What income would your widow (and children) need to live on?   £ .... p.a.
(Ideally you should take what you're living on now and deduct only your personal spending, eg commuting, spending money etc)
less state benefits   £ .... p.a.
less any widow's pension provided by company pension scheme   £ .... p.a.

Grand Total   £ .... p.a.

the type of policy concerned, and partly on your likely life expectancy.

Calculating life expectancy has been honed down to a fine art by the life companies. It is primarily based on age: Table 1 shows the average life expectancy for men and women living in this country, according to the age they are now. While age is the prime factor, the healthiness or otherwise of your way of life naturally has an effect as well, and while for the majority of life policies, companies do not ask you to go along for an individual medical check-up so they can assess your risk with great accuracy, it is common practice these days for proposal forms to include a question relating to smoking, and to 'load' the premiums of smokers.

The younger you are, and the smaller the 'sum assured' (the amount the life company guarantees to pay out on death occurring while the policy is in force) the less stringent the life company will be in assessing you, as it is cheaper for them to work on the average rates. Most companies, however, will have automatic cut-off points after which they will insist you have a medical examination before taking you on. But this 'relaxed' attitude regarding medicals for the young, and to some extent the low premiums, can be expected to change with the relentless spread of AIDS.

Contracts of insurance, incidentally, are in law contracts 'of the utmost good faith'. If you lie on the proposal form,

Table 1
Expectation of Life

Age	Males	Females
20	51.2	57.1
25	46.5	52.2
30	41.7	47.4
35	36.9	42.5
40	32.2	37.7
45	27.6	33.1
50	23.2	28.6
55	19.2	24.3
60	15.5	20.2
65	12.3	16.3
70	9.5	12.8
75	7.4	9.7
80	5.7	7.3
85	4.5	5.6

Table 2
The Cost of Cover

Term Assurance
Sum assured:£25,000

Age next birthday (male)	Annual Premiums		
	3 years	5 years	10 years
30	£32.50	£32.50	£33.00
45	£74.50	£86.50	£115.50
55	£186.00	£225.00	£318.00

Convertible Term
Sum assured: £25,000

Age next birthday (male)	Annual Premiums		
	3 years	5 years	10 years
30	£36.00	£36.00	£37.00
45	£90.00	£100.00	£130.00
55	£233.00	£272.00	£366.00

Convertible Increasable Renewable Term Assurance
Initial Sum assured: £25,000 Initial term: 5 years

Age next birthday (male)	Annual Premiums
30	£60.00
45	£180.00
55	£380.00

Family Income Benefit
Term: 15 years
Annual benefit of £5,000

Age next birthday (male)	Annual Premiums
25	£35
40	£80

Term: 25 years

Age next birthday (male)	Annual Premiums
25	£50
40	£180

the company is entitled to make the contract void and not pay out anything if you die.

Term Assurance

This is the cheapest form of life assurance, and with good reason. The policy lasts for only a set number of years. Should you die in the meantime, the company pays up - but if you survive, there is nothing for you at all and the company 'profits' to the tune of all the premiums you have paid. Given that, at younger ages in particular, the odds of your dying within the next few years are small, the company can afford to charge low premiums for a high sum assured, the premiums of the many going to pay out the sums assured on the few.

Table 2 gives some typical examples of premium rates for different ages, sums assured and terms.

There are several variations available on the basic term assurance policy. First, there is **Decreasing Term Assurance**, where the size of the sum assured decreases to nothing over the term of the policy. This is used in only one situation: to cover the debt outstanding on a mortgage. These are often called Mortgage Protection Policies, and are only required for repayment mortgages: endowment mortgages have their own assurance built into the package.

Then there is **Renewable Term Assurance**. This is more expensive than basic term assurance, because it gives the policy holder the right, at the end of the initial term, to renew his insurance for a further number of years at the normal premium for his age at that time. This right is not necessarily valuable, but it could be: a man of 30, for example, may be in perfect health when he takes out a fifteen-year term policy. But if he suffered a heart attack fourteen years later, he could find that few, if any, companies would be willing to insure him at all in the future, or only at greatly increased rates.

Convertible Term Assurance gives a slightly different right: the right to 'convert' the policy from pure protection to an endowment or whole life policy, again at the normal premium rates for the policy holder's age, no matter what has happened to the state of his health in the meantime.

Finally, there is **Increasable Term Assurance**: the add-on extra here is that policy holders can increase the size of the sum assured (within set limits) on the payment of extra premiums - and that right once again is automatic, however unhealthy you are by that time.

Many policies include all these extras in one package. While straightforward term assurance pays out a lump sum, another type of variation offers a regular income, paid out annually or at more frequent intervals, for a set number of years after a policy holder's death. This is usually called **Family Income Benefit**. The archetypal case for life insurance mentioned earlier - the married man with young children - could probably do with both types: term assurance to pay off the mortgage and other debts, family income benefit to help replace his income.

As far as tax is concerned, any pay-outs made after death are tax-free, whether it is a lump sum or income.

Members of good company pension schemes will find that many of their insurance needs are already covered by the death-in-service benefits of their scheme. It is fairly common to see a lump-sum benefit of three to four times salary at time of death, plus a widow's pension equal to half the pension the member would have been entitled to, if he had made it to retirement. Some schemes pay out special benefits for children as well; rather fewer provide for a widower's pension although that proportion is increasing. Some schemes stop the widow's pension if she re-marries.

If you don't belong to a company scheme, you will have to do it all yourself; but you do at least get some help from the tax system. If you take out your own personal pension, a certain amount of money (not more than 5 per cent of your earnings) can go to buy life assurance, and the premiums qualify for full income tax relief. Even if you cannot, at present, afford to put anything aside for a pension, you can still get the life assurance part of the pension on its own.

Term assurance, in whatever guise, is basically there to take care of the unforeseeable tragedies of life. Other types of life assurance do more. Whole of life policies will pay out when you die (whenever that is) and, if they are 'with-profits' policies, will also acquire a surrender value, meaning that you can cash the policy in before you die, and get something back for your premiums.

Endowment policies last for a set number of years. Should you die in the meantime, the sum assured is paid out; if you survive until the policy matures, you have the prospect of a much larger pay-out. The premiums on both whole life and endowment policies are much higher for any given sum assured than they are for term assurance. Only part of the premiums go to pay for the protection element; the rest is invested on your behalf.

How to Choose the Best Policy

With term assurance, 'shopping around' can be tedious but it's uncomplicated. The legwork is in deciding how much protection you ought to have, and then comparing the fine print of the policies to establish which offer the appropriate extras for you. After that, it is simply a matter of comparing the premium rates for a given sum assured.

Policies that double up as a savings scheme as well as a 'protection' vehicle are a different kettle of fish. You should ask yourself first, do I want or need my savings to go into a life assurance policy - what about the alternatives, ranging from building societies to shares, pension schemes to fine art?

Second, what sort of investment are they providing? Life companies invest their (or rather, our) money in shares, fixed interest securities such as gilts, and property. They do this with varying degrees of success, and it is always advisable to compare the track record of a few companies in the hope of at least avoiding those that appear to be less than competent in the art of investment.

But there is also a great divide over the method of investment. Policies are either 'with-profits' or 'unit-linked'. In the case of the former, all the premiums are pooled into one huge fund. The life company builds up reserves within the fund, to be used to even out the investment returns over good and bad years. The value of a unit-linked policy, on the other hand, is directly linked to the value of the underlying investments.

If your life policy had matured at the end of October 1987, as a with-profits policy holder you would have been completely unaffected by the stock market crash; but if you had a unit-linked policy, its value would have gone down along with everything else.

There is no 'right' answer as to which type of policy to choose, although if you are depending on the proceeds of the policy to pay off your mortgage, there is something to be said for the 'safe and steady' approach of a with-profits policy.

Tax Considerations

If you are using a life assurance policy as a means of saving, it is important to be clear about how the investments are taxed. Life companies can be less than honest in this respect. They state, frequently, that the proceeds of a life policy are 'tax-free'. So they are, as long as you have paid premiums for a minimum number of years (at least ten years, or three-quarters of the original term, if less) and as long as the policy is a 'qualifying' one - which means, basically, that it requires the payment of regular premiums. If one or both of these criteria are not fulfilled, higher rate taxpayers will face some liability to tax, though basic rate taxpayers do not.

However, although the *proceeds* are tax free, the underlying investments have in the meantime been taxed, both as regards income and capital gains. Since the life company pays this tax on your behalf, it is usually 'invisible' and so does not hurt. However, some of the older-style unit-linked policies were set up in such a way that the deductions made for capital gains tax are actually visible: policy holders can see, when their policy matures, the precise amount that has been deducted to pay the CGT. This invariably causes a great outcry from the policy holder who feels he should be able to use his annual exemption from CGT against these gains.

More recent policies don't show this: the price of the units is automatically adjusted to take account of the tax. But while the pocket may not grieve for what the eye does not see, believe me, it is still there. If you do not regularly make full use of your CGT exemption, you should consider carefully whether to use a life assurance plan for your savings: if you used a unit trust instead, you would be able to use your CGT exemption and thus genuinely have 'tax-free' gains.

As far as income is concerned, there is little to choose between the rate at which the life company pays tax, and the basic tax rate for individuals. For higher rate taxpayers, however, a life policy is a tax efficient means of saving - especially if the policy holder is using up his CGT exemption on gains made elsewhere in his portfolio.

These considerations don't apply to term assurance policies as there is no savings element with them.

Policies Written Under Trust

It is common practice these days for policies, particularly term assurance policies, to be written under a trust such as the Married Women's Property Act. The reason is a purely practical one: it means that on death, the proceeds of the policy can be paid out immediately to the beneficiaries, on production of the death certificate; there is no need to wait for probate. Life companies usually have pre-printed forms with the correct wording on them.

Life Assurance and Health

Around 90 per cent of those who fill out proposal forms 'pass', and are accepted at normal premium rates for their age. If you have a history of bad health, however, you should not leap to the conclusion that you are uninsurable. Life companies are often only one step behind the doctors in the matter of medical knowledge, and some conditions, which only a few years ago might have led to a complete refusal for insurance purposes, are now happily accepted by insurance companies. A breast cancer operation, for example, or a heart attack, no longer mean lives are uninsurable.

It does, however, mean that the life company will consult your own doctor, and possibly ask you to go along for an independent medical check-up as well. Depending on results, the premiums may be higher than normal, and the company may also impose a 'debt' on the policy for a number of years.

This means that if you drop dead before the 'debt' term is up, the company will not pay out the whole of the sum assured. This procedure can be useful if you need a life assurance policy as part of a tax-planning package.

Some insurance brokers are specialists in arranging life assurance for 'impaired lives' and if you are in this position, it would be well worth seeking their advice. The British Insurance and Investment Brokers Association (see end of chapter) can point you in the appropriate direction.

There may be some situations where there is a much easier solution. Suppose, for example, a married couple has an endowment mortgage which they now need to increase substantially. If the husband as suffered a heart attack, say, the usual 'joint life, first death' endowment policy may involve loaded premiums. If he already has substantial life assurance through his company pension scheme, why not simply take out the new endowment policy in the wife's name only? - The premiums are likely to be a good bit lower anyway, given that women live longer than men on average, a fact reflected in normal premium rates.

Early Surrender

Term policies cannot be surrendered; you can stop paying the premiums, the cover will be withdrawn, and that's it. With whole life and endowment policies, however, you can surrender them before their term is up (or before you die) and get something back for your pains. In the early years of a policy, however, the something is unlikely to be very much.

All the expenses of setting up a policy - the administration, the underwriting and, by no means least, the commission payable to the salesman - are paid for out of the first premiums you pay. This can mean that, even a couple of years into a policy, there is precious little to show for your money. So if you possibly can, avoid getting into a situation where you are forced to surrender a policy. That means, one, making sure you are not making too high a commitment in the first place (don't be over-persuaded by the salesman) and two, if you really can't afford the premiums, or need the money, considering the other alternatives to surrender. These are:

1. Make the policy 'paid up'. This means you no longer have to pay any premiums, but the policy remains in force until the end of the original term (with a reduced sum assured). This will at least give you something back for your money.

2. If you need a lump sum now, see if you can borrow against the policy. Some life companies are prepared to make loans against their own policies, and often at fairly reasonable interest rates.

3. Or you can try selling your policy. One company holds regular auctions of life policies; the 'reserve price' will always be set higher than the surrender value, so you do not lose out. Another organisation has recently been set up to buy life policies - for details, see end of chapter.

Other Types of Life Assurance Policies

With whole life and more especially endowment policies, the 'protection' element is heavily mixed up with a savings element as well. Single premium life assurance policies go one step further; they are almost totally investment-orientated contracts, with a 'sum assured' which is usually no more than the amount of the premium you have paid. They are dealt with in detail in Chapter Five.

Coming back to the protection side, there is also **Permanent Health Insurance (PHI)**. These policies will pay out a regular income if you fall ill and hence are unable to work. Employees with a good sick-pay scheme are unlikely to be interested; for the self-employed, however, a PHI policy may be just as important as life assurance.

The cost of a PHI policy depends on your age, your health history, the amount of income you are insuring (most companies will stipulate a maximum of, say, 75 per cent of your earnings) and the length of the *deferred period*. This is the length of time that must elapse between the onset of illness and the time the policy starts paying out. The minimum offered is four weeks - you won't find any company willing to cough up every time you catch a cold and decide to stay in bed for a few days - and the maximum deferred period offered is usually one year. Since the chance of anyone being ill and unable to work for more than a year is considerably less than a one-month period, the premiums are correspondingly much cheaper.

Finally, premiums for women are considerably higher than for men - as much as 50 per cent more. This is because, the life companies claim, the statistics show that while women enjoy lower mortality rates than men, they have much higher *morbidity* rates (propensity to be ill).

If you decide you need a PHI policy, you should also look closely at any exclusions in the policy wording: most policies do not pay out for illnesses arising from drug or alcohol abuse, or from pregnancy; others have a much longer list of exclusions.

Home and Contents Insurance

Until you pay off your mortgage, you have no control over the fact that your property is insured, and little control over how, and with whom, the insurance is effected. Lenders insist that your home (the security for their loan) is insured to its full value, that the insurance is kept in force and index-linked, and will usually choose the insurance company as well. Borrowers have a right to ask for another company if they wish, but lenders have the last word: unless the policy is adequate in their view, they may turn it down. In any case, many will make an 'administrative charge' for such a freedom - £25 is typical.

Premiums for the insurance are usually collected monthly, along with the mortgage payment. Once the mortgage is completed, it becomes your responsibility to keep the insurance in force. The premiums for the policy depend on the estimated re-building costs, which are generally taken from a survey conducted annually by the Royal Institution of Chartered Surveyors. Typical premium rates at present are around £1.80 per £1,000 sum insured.

Policies differ in their small print, and it is important to find out whether, for example, damage to garden sheds is included; or the cost of alternative accommodation should your house be uninhabitable, or whether there is an 'excess' (an amount the policy holder must pay out of his own pocket first) on damage resulting from subsidence.

While the total sum assured is index-linked, it will not automatically be increased to reflect the extra value of any additions or improvements you may make to the house. You should inform the insurance company of any major items here, otherwise you could be under-insured, giving the insurer the right to scale down any pay-outs to you by a similar proportion.

The Association of British Insurers (for address see end of chapter) publishes several free leaflets on home insurance.

Insurance of contents is your own responsibility. Premium rates have been soaring in recent years, particularly for policy holders living in 'high risk' areas, notably the larger cities. Despite this, insurance companies are still making losses on this aspect of their business, so the premiums are likely to rise still further.

There is little point in shopping around just to try to find cheaper rates. Insurers continually re-classify their areas of low and high risk according to their claims experience, and you may be lucky one year by finding that your district is rated lower by one company than by another. But that advantage is unlikely to continue for more than a year or so.

However - at last - insurance companies are beginning to be a bit more imaginative. Some of them have realised that there are reasonably effective deterrents to burglary: alarm systems, membership of neighbourhood watch schemes, or the likelihood of there being someone around the house most of the day. Some policies offer discounts to homeowners with a burglar alarm system or to policy holders who are retired. One even offers a discount to homeowners with dogs. 'No claims bonuses' are just beginning to appear.

When you choose your policy, do remember to look for any extras you might need – insurance for the contents of your freezer, for instance, for accidental damage or for 'all risks' insurance for movable items such as cameras and bicycles. You must insure the full value of your property, otherwise, as with buildings insurance, the company has the right to scale down its pay-outs. Many policies require you to declare any single item forming more than 5 per cent of the total sum insured; you may be charged extra.

Some building societies offer packages of house and contents insurance all in one. These can be good value but will not suit everyone: in many cases, the total sum assured for the contents is automatically set at a high level, often identical to the amount the building is insured for.

Complaints and Cautionary Tales

Most insurance companies belong to the Insurance Ombudsman Bureau, an independent body whose purpose in life is to provide a neutral hearing-ground to resolve complaints between companies and their policy holders. Chapter Eleven gives more details of how the scheme works.

The Ombudsman's report is published annually, giving details of the cases he has had to consider over the year, and it usually contains a few pertinent lessons for the rest of us.

One problem that continually crops up is the mistaken assumption of policy holders that the terms of their policy will remain completely unchanged for as long as they pay the premiums. This is not necessarily the case. The insurance contract is a yearly one; at the end of that time, the insurer can make any changes he likes to the terms of cover offered. He must, of course, inform the policy holder of any change; and the policy holder is, of course, quite free to turn it down and go elsewhere. The problem is, though, that people tend to ignore any official looking bumpf from their insurance company and so are quite unaware of the fact that the terms of cover may have deteriorated since they originally chose that company's policy.

Another typical source of complaint is what can be called the 'three piece suite' scenario. Suppose you have a matching settee and two armchairs, one of which is damaged and has to be replaced. What if you cannot find one to match the rest? Are you entitled to claim for the whole suite? The answer is, probably not.

There can be many 'borderline' cases along these lines, which cannot possibly be catered for in the small print of the policy. Sometimes the balance may tip towards the policy holder, but sometimes not.

Buying Insurance

Anyone called themselves an 'insurance broker' must be registered with the Insurance Brokers Registration Council. Individuals must have a professional qualification or appropriate experience, and have to convince the Council as to their 'character and suitability' to be a broker. They should also follow a code of conduct which enjoins them, among other things, to 'place the interests of their client above all other considerations' (such as the commission they might be paid). If a large part of their business is advising on investments as well as insurance, they should also be members of the Financial Intermediaries, Managers and Brokers Association.

The British Insurance and Investment Brokers Association (BIIBA) is the trade association for insurance brokers. It can provide names and addresses of its members, and can also advise on firms which specialise in unusual business – insurance for 'impaired lives', for example; insurance for thatched cottages, or vintage cars. BIIBA runs an informal conciliation service for complaints that arise between individuals and brokers (the Insurance Ombudsman deals with insurance companies, not brokers) and if you have a serious complaint concerning a broker, you should also go to the IBRC.

There is no need to buy your insurance through a broker. You can always go direct to the company concerned, the one exception being policies underwritten at Lloyd's, which can only be approached via a broker. Buying direct, however, does not save money.

Diana Wright

Information and Contacts
Insurance Brokers Registration Council
15 St Helen's Place
London EC3A 6DS
01-588 4387

British Insurance & Investment Brokers Association
14 Bevis Marks
London EC3A 7NT
01-623 9043

Association of British Insurers
Aldermary House
Queen Street
London EC4N 1TU
01-248 4477

Insurance Ombudsman Bureau
31 Southampton Row
London WC1B 5HJ
01-242 8613

Alternatives to Surrendering Life Policies
Foster & Cranfield (Auctioneers) 01-608 1941
The Policy Network 01-929 2971

9 On Retirement

Joints may crack louder and 500 yards make a mile, but next to health the big problem in retirement is income. Happiness when the wage packets stop is not having to worry too much about the next fuel bill.

The lucky ones have a good pension from their ex-employers, a bit more from the state and a clutch of investments to provide more security.

If you are less well off, you may have to make out with a part-time job or freelance your professional skills.

The commonest of all financial questions before and after retirement is 'What should I do with my money?' It would be nice if there were an equally common answer, but unfortunately there isn't. Everyone's problem is different and needs its own solution. Like the chemist's shop, however, the investment industry has a shelf of ingredients from which the right mixture can be put together to suit each individual.

At no time is it more important to take stock of your financial position than it is at retirement. The house you live in may be tying up much-needed capital, while your savings and investments, though happily ticking up growth, may need to be put to a different use, to produce income.

In short, once you retire your assets need a thorough over-haul and adjustment to meet your changed circumstances. The range of investments available makes it possible to do this in the most efficient way. The principal choices, which are sufficient for most people, are outlined in the next few pages.

Annuities

Many people these days reach retirement age with a lump sum to invest. It may come from a matured insurance policy, commuted occupational pension, the profit from moving to a cheaper house, a portfolio of investments or an everyday nest egg in the building society.

The better off have more than one cash sum to collect at the end of their working lives. For many others, especially those with no occupational pension, savings and any other cash they may be able to muster may have to be used to provide immediate maximum income.

One way to do this is to buy an ordinary annuity. This will provide at the outset better income than a fixed rate investment, but there are drawbacks.

The principal one is that once you sign up for a lifetime income you can never change your mind and get your money back. Buying an annuity is gambling that you will live long enough to get your money's worth. With a normal contract, if you die a couple of days after handing over your cheque nothing comes back to your dependants.

It goes instead to subsidise the longer stayers. Without the unused money left by those who die early, the insurance company would not be able to pay such high rates.

However, although you will never see your capital again, you can, if you are prepared to give up some of your income, ensure that part of your money is returned to your dependants if you die within a stipulated period, usually five years.

Because you are likely to die relatively more quickly, the older you are at the time you take out the annuity, the better the income you will get. So the purchase of an annuity should be put off as long as possible. The rate applying at the outset holds good throughout, and for this reason it is best to buy when interest rates are high.

Even so, annuities vary from one insurance company to another, and this is one of those occasions when it is particularly advisable to ask around, or keep in touch with one of the financial magazines like *Planned Savings* or *Money Management* which regularly quote current rates.

Like everyone else on fixed incomes, a constant worry for annuitants is inflation. In exchange for part of your starting income you can protect yourself to some extent by having your payments increased annually. If inflation is high, however, it is impracticable to try to combat it in this way.

If you are married, the annuity contract should be written on a joint basis so that the income extends over both lives.

A plus point for annuities is that part of the income is agreed by the Inland Revenue as repayment of capital, and this part is not subject to tax.

Income and Investment Bonds

Like annuities, though in a different way, investment bonds are a bit of a gamble. With these, you stake your money on the movement of interest rates.

Bonds come in a number of varieties. With some, brokers split your money between a specially negotiated building society account and a unit trust or managed fund – a combination of gilt-edged, property and equity investment – or some other second leg as the marketing fancy takes them.

The building society part, with a premium interest rate usually guaranteed for a year, is really a carrot to tempt investors into the longer-term investment (the building society account can be cashed in after the year or retained at a new interest rate). It does give the total investment a good send-off, but it is the subsequent performance of the risk investment that counts.

Building societies have their own fixed-rate bonds – not to be confused with guaranteed premium accounts. The former offer an interest rate guaranteed to stay the same for a year, the latter guarantee to pay a percentage over the changeable ordinary share rate.

Some insurance companies offer investments pledged to maintain income for stated periods, usually between one and five years. Advertisements for these guaranteed income bonds usually appear when interest rates are going down.

All guaranteed rates, of course, are worth considering only if you think market rates are not likely to move higher. The bond is a winner only if other rates go down, but this is one decision where a financial adviser can't be of much help. Your guess is as good as his.

Building Societies

In a fiercely competitive market building societies now have to offer savers a much better deal than they once got away with. Although they are deeply into the wider field of financial services, their main function is still to take in money to re-lend to home-buyers.

They are able to go to the money markets for 40 per cent of this, but for the bulk of the money they need they have to rely on the small saver and the attraction of their high interest accounts. These are built around a permutated system of withdrawal terms, penalties, how much cash is deposited and for how long.

Every high street has its display of percentage signs, and there is never much to choose between them. The real bargains are less conspicuous and are to be found among the smaller societies. Although their rates move up and down with the rest of the market, they manage to maintain an edge over what is available from their bigger brethren.

There is some loss of convenience in dealing with a smaller society. As they have few branches, business must usually be done through the post.

Watch for the catch with extra interest accounts. The rate you think you are getting may not be as high as it seems. It is not always possible to give the necessary notice, usually three months, and that period of interest is lost on money withdrawn. Some deduct interest whether or not notice is given if the balance falls below a specified amount, which means that at some point in time you are a certain loser unless you leave your money with the society forever.

When you are opting for a scheme where withdrawal notice is required, try to keep one step ahead of the game. If interest rates look like going up within the term of the notice period, it is worth giving immediate notice so that you will have your cash on hand for a quick transfer.

If you are a non-taxpayer remember the building societies deduct tax at basic rate from your interest, and you can't reclaim it. The only deposit-taking institution that pays interest gross is the Department for National Savings. Unit trust dividends are paid net of tax, but the tax is reclaimable.

National Savings

For retired people needing regular payments the Department for National Savings has an offer worth considering. Its Income Bonds pay interest monthly and it is paid in full without deducting tax. This is a big plus for non-taxpayers. Other institutions such as the banks and building societies must deduct income tax at the prevailing basic rate from everyone's interest, and it is not reclaimable.

Income bonds are sold in multiples of £1,000 and the minimum holding is £2,000. Payments are made on the fifth of each month after the bond has been held for six weeks. The rate varies with market changes but six weeks' notice is given of any change. This works in the saver's favour if the rate is coming down, but it means he has to wait that long before he gets the benefit of any increase.

For withdrawal of capital three months' notice is necessary, and on money withdrawn within the first year the interest is halved. After that there is no penalty.

Banks
Like the building societies, the high street banks offer a range of savings accounts, the commonest being the seven-day deposit account which requires that period of notice. This carries a low rate of interest with higher rates available for longer-term money.

Bank accounts should be used strategically. Few people these days are financially unwise enough to keep more in their current accounts that necessary to meet regular commitments. The banks recognise this and feel under no obligation to pay interest on outstanding balances.

What they do instead is to encourage transfers of spare cash into deposit accounts. When your current account runs down to the danger level the bank can automatically top it up from your deposit account, so making sure you don't inadvertently incur bank charges. Longer-term cash can go into a higher interest account.

In addition to the normal deposit accounts, the commercial banks issue certificates of deposit. These are bearer documents which can be sold to third parties. Interest is fixed for the term of the certificate - normally between three and five years. CD's usually require a high minimum investment.

Unit Trusts
More than 120 unit trusts are structured for people who need income which doesn't get left behind by inflation.

Capital invested at fixed interest rates never grows so long as income is taken from it. Income unit trusts aim to increase both income and capital. This, of course, takes time so the initial income is not as high as that from a high rate fixed-interest account.

In time, the income from a unit trust should outstrip that from a building society where the capital remains static in nominal terms and in fact reduces in real value as a result of inflation.

Unit trusts, of course, as the stock market collapse in October 1987 was a painful reminder, are risk investments, but on long-term form they have proved to be a good defence against inflation.

Income is paid net of basic rate tax, which means that if you are a higher rate taxpayer you will have to make up the difference. If on the other hand you do not pay tax, unlike a bank or building society deduction, you can reclaim it.

You can specify the income you require from a unit trust investment, always remembering that the more income you take the less you leave for capital growth. It may mean dipping into your capital when yields are low.

Unit-Linked Bonds

These are insurance policies in name but investments in practice. All but a fraction of your money goes into a unit trust and the actual life cover is minimal – usually the amount of your investment. Companies offer a choice of funds and you can move your money from one to another in line with changing market conditions.

Up to 5 per cent of your original investment may be withdrawn each year tax-free. The insurance company is responsible for your income tax at basic rate and any capital gains tax, but if you are a higher rate taxpayer you may have something to pay later. If you are a non-taxpayer you cannot reclaim any tax allowed for by the company.

As with an ordinary unit trust, the return depends on how the underlying fund performs. A bond of this kind is probably unsuitable for you in retirement unless you are likely to be paying tax at higher rates for a few years. The advantage is that it allows you to defer tax on withdrawals until you cash-in the whole policy, by which time your rate may be lower.

Government Stocks

Gilt-edged securities can guarantee your income, but not necessarily the full return of your capital. Gilts are traded on the stock market and prices fluctuate from day to day, so you might make a capital profit or a loss, depending on your buying and selling prices.

The interest on a government stock, however, never alters, so your income is secured from the time you buy regardless of how the price moves.

You can invest in gilts through a stockbroker, your bank or your local main post office, the last-named being the cheapest. There are more than enough stocks to choose from on the National Savings Stock Register. They are listed in a leaflet available at the post office.

Gilts come in three varieties – shorts, mediums and longs – according to whether the Government is due to redeem them in under five years, five to fifteen years, or over fifteen. In retirement you will probably find the short-dated stocks most suitable. The nearer a stock is to redemption, the less volatile the price fluctuations are likely to be, as it will gradually move closer towards the par value (£100) at which the Government repays it.

By applying on a post office form to the Bonds and Stock Office at Blackpool, you save on stockbroker dealing costs, and if you are a non-taxpayer you will be happy to know that your income is paid gross. A snag is that it takes several days to process your application and you may find that the deal has been put through for you at a higher price that you thought.

Another drawback is that by going it alone you cut yourself off from expert advice. This is particularly important where gilts are concerned, as the timing of both buying and selling is crucial.

Income from your Home

The time may come when your income fails to meet your needs or to provide the little extras that make all the difference to life after work. If you own your own home, selling up and moving to a cheaper property is one way of putting some money in the bank. Most people, however, especially when they are nearing the age of 70, do not wish to give up their home or move away from friends and relatives. Many have found the answer in a home income plan. This is a type of scheme which allows you to make use of the capital tied up in your home without having to move out. There are several variants, but the basic home income plan involves taking a loan on the value of the house and using it to buy income for life in the form of an annuity.

From this, interest on the loan is paid, and the remainder

is spending money. The loan itself is repaid from the proceeds when the house is eventually sold. In the meantime you have the right to live in it for as long as you and your wife or husband live.

Before entering into a contract of this kind, consult your nearest relatives. Elderly people are often reluctant to use up assets they wish to leave to their children. However, few children would not prefer to see struggling parents use their house equity to ease their final years.

As time goes on, the value of the property will increase. The surplus may be left to build up for your heirs - or some of it may be used to increase your income.

As explained previously in this chapter (see *Annuities*), the older you are the higher the income you receive from an annuity. For this reason, a home income plan is not considered to be worthwhile for anyone much under the age of 70, or for couples with joint ages of 150, although 145 may be accepted. The size of the loan depends on the value of the property but you are not likely to get more than 80 per cent of the property value, and the limit is £30,000 - the level at which tax relief on the interest stops. You may, however, take a smaller loan, but any later topping up will incur charges.

A woman receives less income than a man of the same age. This is because she is expected to live longer, so the annuity payments are spread over a longer period. It also explains why the income for couples is also lower than for a single man, as it has to run for both lifetimes.

The loan repayment rate may be fixed throughout, or it may vary with market rates. The fixed rate is usually set comparatively low and will probably turn out to be better than the average variable rate over the period of the mortgage. Whichever way general rates go it ensures that you know exactly what your income is going to be from one month to the next.

Reversion Schemes
The difference between a mortgage scheme and a reversion scheme is that with the first you retain *possession* of your home, with the second you sell it to the company but retain *occupation* as a tenant at a nominal rent.

The amount you receive will probably be around half the market value of the property. It may be paid as a lump sum or as an annuity. The house passes to the company only when you die, and the company also receives any increase in value.

One reason why some people opt for a reversion instead of a mortgage scheme is that the age limit is lower, depending on the company. One company will accept people aged 60, but the younger you are the lower the price you will get for your home. As there is no loan interest to pay, however, the net income will be higher from a given gross amount with a reversion scheme.

One type of reversion scheme allows you to retain an interest in your property. In exchange for lower income, you need sell only part of the property, and more as you get older to take advantage of higher annuity rates. In the meantime you will share in any increase in value.

Another variant involves pooling your property with others. The starting income depends on your age and the value of your home. It then increases with the rise in value of all properties in the scheme, which is open to people aged 60. If you die in the first year, your beneficiaries receive 75 per cent of the house value.

Professional advice is essential with all schemes involving the sale or mortgaging of your home. An expert appraisal of your circumstances is necessary, including the tax implications and possible effect on any social security benefits you may have. In addition to a solicitor, a specialist broker is advisable to decide which, if any, scheme is suitable for you. Some useful names and addresses are given at the end of this chapter.

Without a Will

Laying down who gets what when you die is not a pleasant task, and many people put it off until it is too late. They die without leaving any clear instructions as to how they wish their possessions to be split up - in legal jargon, intestate. Instead of their assets going to those they would most like to have them, they are distributed in accordance with a set of rules.

You should never feel that your wishes are so self-evident or your assets so meagre that it is a waste of time making a will. Your house alone could be the subject of bitter family squabbles, or you could die just as an unexpected windfall comes your way, such as a big Premium Bond prize.

The intestacy rules are designed for general fairness, but they don't reflect the wishes of individuals. Briefly, if you die without leaving a will your assets will be divided as follows:

Widow with No Children: She receives the first £85,000 of your property plus all your personal possessions such as the car, furniture etc. She also gets a half share of the remainder of your estate, the other half going to your parents if still alive. Otherwise to any of your brothers or sisters or their children.

Widow with Children: She receives the first £40,000 plus chattels and a life share in half of the remaining assets. Children receive the other part immediately, and when their mother dies the first half.

No Spouse: The estate is divided equally among the children. If one of your children died before you, his children receive what he would have got.

No Spouse or Children: The estate passes to any of your surviving parents, otherwise to brothers and sisters. Next come their children, then any surviving grandparents, followed by aunts and uncles. If no heir is found everything goes to the Crown. Common law wives or husbands are not provided for in the pecking order, but they can apply to the court for 'reasonable provision'.

It all sounds reasonable enough, but suppose you and your wife have a fatal road accident. If your wife lives just one hour longer than you, that is sufficient for your estate to pass to her. In which case if you have no children it all passes to her parents instead of yours.

There is nothing to stop you making a will on your own, which is certainly better than none at all. Special forms can be bought from stationers, but it is much better to go to a solicitor who is able to see legal snags that may escape you. It takes very little time to draw up a normal will and the cost is not high. The solicitor is best able also to make any alterations to the will which you may wish to make later.

The solicitor can also act as executor to carry out your wishes. He will probably charge much less than the trustee department of a bank or insurance company, and will provide a more personal service. You can appoint in addition a friend or member of the family as an executor.

A good reason for putting your affairs in the hands of professionals is that they may save your heirs inheritance tax. Provided you give them the necessary discretion, your executors should be able to adjust your original instructions to meet unforeseen conditions.

An alternative to a discretionary will is a deed of family arrangement, under which beneficiaries may agree to vary the provision of the will for tax purposes. The arrangement can be made at any time within two years of your death, but this is something of an emergency measure and less efficient than a discretionary will.

Tax and Tenancy

Inheritance tax is charged at 40 per cent on assets over a specified amount, but they can be distributed in ways to avoid unnecessary payments.

Apart from any other assets, your home could put you in the potential inheritance tax bracket. There is no problem if you are leaving the house or your share in it to your wife or husband, because no inheritance tax is payable on assets passing between spouses. The problem arises when the second partner dies, if no defensive action has been taken.

There are two ways for couples to own their home jointly. One is by a joint tenancy and the other as tenants in common. Where there is no threat of inheritance tax, the simplest way is the more common joint tenancy. Under this the house passes automatically to the surviving partner.

If a tax liability is likely, however, the tenancy in common may be best. This gives each partner a clearly defined share of the house, rather than a joint ownership of the whole. Normally the share would be a straight half each, but it can be split into other fractions.

What a tenancy in common does is to allow either partner to dispose of his or her share while still alive and so remove that amount from the estate. The idea is to reduce the estate closer to or below the inheritance tax threshold, if possible.

If you are handing over your share of the property to your son or daughter, be careful about making any stipulations such as retaining the right to use the house as though it were still yours. The taxman has an answer to those who make gifts in name only. Under the 'gifts with reservations' rule he can disallow gifts for tax purposes which he believes are not genuine. One way of satisfying him is to show that you have been paying rent for continuing to live in the property.

If you wish at any time to make a completely new will, make sure that the old one is destroyed in your presence. Keep the new one in a safe (but sensible) place so that your executors don't have to strip the walls and tear up the floorboards to find it. Your bank will hold it with any other valuable documents for a small annual charge.

While it may be known that you made a valid will, if it can't be found you will be deemed to have died intestate.

State Pension

Once you reach retirement age (65 man, 60 woman), you will be entitled to a state pension, provided you have made the necessary contributions. The pension comes in two parts – the basic pension and an additional payment related to your earnings.

To get the full basic pension you need to have paid National Insurance contributions for most years of your working life – roughly nine out of ten. To qualify as a pensionable year a certain number of contributions must be either made or credited. Working life is the period between age 16 to retirement, or from the time the National Insurance scheme started in 1948.

If your income is below what you need to live on you may apply for 'pension premium', but only if you have less than £8,000 in savings. If you have between £3,000 and £8,000 you will get only a scaled-down benefit.

This includes building society deposits, savings certificates and even Premium bonds, but not the value of your home or personal possessions. There is more money for a couple over 60 and where one partner is over 80.

Additional help with up to 80 per cent of your rates may be claimed, but you get no help with your water rates.

Working After Retirement

The state pension does not come automatically. You have to apply for it, and before it is granted the DHSS will have to be satisfied that you have actually retired from full-time work – not just reached retirement age. If not you will have to defer your pension.

Voluntary deferment may be worthwhile if you have a part-time job or other income sufficient to enable you to do without the pension for a while. The benefit is twofold.

First, the pension would otherwise be reduced in line with your earnings over a specified amount; second, the longer you put off drawing it, the higher it will be when you finally decide to take it.

You can defer your pension until you reach the age of 70. After that it must be taken, but by then it will have increased at the rate of around 7.5 per cent a year in addition to the usual index-linked annual increases.

You may then be ready to give up your part-time work and settle down to real retirement, but if not the pension will no longer be subject to the 'earnings rule'. Under this, you are allowed to earn only £75 a week. On the next £4 you lose 5p of your pension for every 10p earned, and after that 10p for every 10p, until your pension is cancelled out altogether. Remember also that it is taxed along with your other income.

The good news is that once you reach retirement age you do not have to pay national insurance on your earnings, and the earnings rule applies only to the basic state pension, not the earnings-related part or any occupational pension.

If you have been drawing your pension then decide to go back to full-time work, you can cancel it and allow it to increase until you retire finally. If your wife has a pension on your contributions, she will have to give it up. To avoid paying NI contributions, you will need a certificate of age exemption from your local social security office. Ask for Form CF 384. You can only cancel retirement once.

If you have a full contributions record you may be able to retire early without losing any of your state pension, although this is payable only at retirement age. Otherwise you can pay voluntary contributions to preserve your rights. Check with your social security office.

Joe Irving

Information and Contacts
Home Income Plans

Hinton & Wild (Insurance) Ltd
374–378 Ewell Road
Surbiton
Surrey KT6 7BB

Allied Dunbar plc
9-15 Sackville Street
London W1X 1DE

Home Reversions Ltd
30 Windsor Place
Cardiff CF1 3UR

Stalwart Assurance Co Ltd
Tuition House
St George's Road
Wimbledon
London SW19 4XE

Booklets
Using your home as capital
Your rights: A guide to money benefits for retired people

Both published by Age Concern - Bernard Sunley House, 60
Pitcairn Road, Mitcham, Surrey CR4 3LL

Magazines
Money Management, Greystoke Place, Fetter Lane,
London EC4A 1ND

Planned Savings, 33-35 Bowling Green Lane,
London EC1R 0DA

10 Tax and Tax Planning

'To tax and to please, no more than to love and be wise, is not given to men'. So said Edmund Burke, 18th-century politician and philosopher, so proving that there's little essential about human life that the passage of a mere century or two can change.

Some people will go to any lengths to avoid tax, others to avoid thinking about it. Neither is an easy goal to attain, although the Inland Revenue do try hard to make the latter aim achievable (and the former impossible).

People on Pay As You Earn (PAYE) who are liable to no more than basic rate income tax may not hear from their tax office for years on end. However pleasant a state this is, there is a fundamental point about paying tax to bear in mind: it is your duty to make sure the Revenue have all the information necessary to assess your tax liability correctly and saying 'they didn't ask me for it' is no excuse for why you didn't pay.

There are three major taxes that impinge on the life of an individual: income tax, Capital Gains Tax (CGT) and Inheritance Tax (IHT). This chapter deals in brief with all three. It cannot possibly go into all the details of how the taxes work, or of the complicated schemes devised by tax experts to minimise their effect. Further reading can be useful, and if you have a large and complex tax problem to solve, competent professional advice is essential.

Table 1 shows the main tax facts and figures for the fiscal year 1988-89. Thanks to a 500-year-old accident of history, tax years run from the 6th of April each year to the 5th of April the following year.

Income Tax

There are now just two rates of income tax: 25 per cent (the basic rate) and a higher rate of 40 per cent. At present, it makes no difference how the income was earned - whether from your job or your investments (the latter often referred to as 'unearned' income). The rates are fixed for bands of

Table 1
Tax facts and figures 1988–89

Income Tax Rates

Taxable Income	Rate (%)
£1-£19,300	25
£19,301 upwards	40

Personal Allowances

Single person's allowance	£2,605
Married man's allowance	£4,095
Wife's earned income allowance	£2,605
Additional personal allowance	£1,490
Widow's bereavement allowance	£1,490
Age allowance:	
Single (under 80)	£3,180★
Married (under 80)	£5,035★
Single (80 or over)	£3,310★
Married (80 or over)	£5,205★
Blind Person's allowance	£540

Capital Gains Tax
Tax is charged at either 25% or 40%, depending on the investor's marginal
rate of income tax for that year, on net taxable gains above £5,000.

Inheritance Tax

Running total of taxable gifts	Lifetime rate (%)	Death rate (%)
£0–£110,000	Nil	Nil
£110,001 upwards	20	40

★The extra age allowance is progressively withdrawn once total income
exceeds £10,600.

taxable income, that is, after any tax-free allowances and tax
deductible expenses you may have.

The personal allowances, shown in the table, are index-
linked and so will rise automatically each year in line with
the cost of living - or more, if a Chancellor decides on a
give-away budget.

A good general principle in all your tax affairs is to let
your tax office know of any changes in your circumstances
as soon as possible - for example, if you become old enough
for age allowance - so that there's no delay in getting any
extra relief you may be entitled to. There is, in any case, a
time limit imposed on getting any money back if you have
been overpaying: the clock runs out six years after you have
paid the tax.

In addition to the allowances, there are certain tax deductible
expenses you can claim. The principle ones for employees are:

1. Mortgage Interest Relief

This is limited to interest on loans up to £30,000 used for the purpose of buying your principal place of residence. Note that interest is usually paid net of basic rate tax relief, though higher rate relief must be specifically claimed. Remember that it is also available for interest on bridging loans used to purchase your new home, and in this case you will probably be paying the interest gross.

2. Pension Contributions

No matter what type of pension scheme you have – company or personal – any contributions you make are tax deductible, up to specified limits (see Chapter Seven for details).

3. Covenants

A deed of covenant is an undertaking you make to pay regular annual amounts to someone or something – an individual or a charity, for example. The agreement must be capable, in law, of exceeding six years, or three years in the case of a charity.

Covenants to an individual have no significance for tax these days, but covenants to a charity do. A charity can re-claim from the Revenue an amount equal to the basic rate of tax on your gift, while higher rate taxpayers can claim back for themselves the higher rate tax.

Anyone who is self-employed or running their own business is likely to have a great many other items that he can claim against his gross income: expenses that are 'wholly and exclusively' incurred in the running of the business may be offset.

This is obviously only a quick skate through the labyrinth of income tax regulations.

Further Information

The following publications are most useful:

The Allied Dunbar Tax Guide, published by Longmans. 1987–8 edition cost £12.95; edition for current tax year usually published around August.

The Which? Book of Tax, published by the Consumers' Association and Hodder & Stoughton. 1987–8 edition cost £9.95. *The Which? Tax Saving Guide* is published each March as part of the magazine *Which?* It is not available separately but should be in your local library.

The Inland Revenue publish a range of leaflets on various aspects of income tax including: Personal Allowances (IR22); Income Tax and Widows (IR23); Income Tax: Wife's Earnings Election (IR13); Income Tax: Age Allowance (IR4); Income Tax and Pensioners (IR4A); Income Tax: Separation and Divorce (IR30). All available free from local enquiry offices.

Income Tax Planning Points
Tax and Marriage: Separate Taxation
If you and your partner earn more than £28,484 between you during 1988-9, then it can be beneficial to opt for separate taxation. The man loses his extra married man's tax allowance, but the overall tax payable is less because both partners can make full use of the basic rate band. The minimum the lower paid partner must earn is currently £6,579. Note that these figures will automatically change each year as personal allowances (and possibly tax rates) change: most newspapers will carry the new figures somewhere in their Budget coverage, and *The Which? Tax Saving Guide* invariably includes full details. Separate taxation only applies to earned income: any unearned income of a wife is currently automatically treated as her husband's.

How and when to elect for separate taxation: You need to fill out form 14 from the Revenue and both sign within twelve months after the end of the tax year in which you are claiming it.

Tax and Marriage from 1990
At long last, the tax system is about to edge away from its Victorian past, and the assumption that women neither deserved nor were capable of being taxpayers in their own right. From 1990, a new system of taxation is being brought in for married couples which will, among other things, make the business of deciding whether or not to opt for separate taxation a thing of the past.

The new system of independent taxation will give each partner a full personal allowance to use against any kind of income - earned or unearned. Partner's incomes will automatically be separately taxed. In addition to the ordinary personal allowance, there will also be a 'married couple's allowance' (equal to the difference between the single person's and married man's allowance). This will automatically go to the husband, unless he has insufficient income, in which case any unused part can be transferred to the wife.

Also, under the new system, each partner will be entitled to have his or her own exemption against Capital Gains Tax – currently £5,000 – instead of having to share one between them, as at present.

Tax and Divorce
Divorce and permanent separation are treated practically the same for income tax purposes. The taxman used to give a helping hand with maintenance payments, but this has now been largely withdrawn. Until the 1988 Budget, payers could get tax relief on their maintenance payments, and while this was in theory 'taxable income' in the hands of the recipient, in many cases no tax was actually payable as it could be set against personal allowances.

Anyone who had a maintenance agreement in force at the time of the Budget is not immediately affected by the new rules. For those getting divorced now, however, there is no help at all from the Revenue. No tax relief is available for those who pay the maintenance, although the quid pro quo is that the payments are no longer taxable (even in theory) in the hands of the recipient.

Those who are already divorced will have the amount of tax relief to which they are entitled 'frozen' at 1987–8 levels.

Tax and Age
Once you reach the age of 65 you are entitled to an extra personal allowance known as the age allowance – and if you make it to 80, it's even higher, as the table shows. But the Revenue's generosity is limited and once your income exceeds a certain level the extra allowance is progressively withdrawn at the rate of £2 for every £3 extra income, until it is extinguished completely. If your income is in the vulnerable band, you are effectively a 'higher rate taxpayer' and a rearrangement of your investments may help to preserve some or all of the extra allowances. (See the section on tax and investments below).

Tax and Investments

Some investments actually reduce your income tax bill which is an added incentive (though should not be a reason on its own) to invest. Others can be particularly tax efficient for investors. A few are both. Unless you are an expert yourself, it is always wise to seek professional advice, but it is more important with some investments than with others. A star rating on the need for advice (one star means not important: three means essential) is given below.

1. Pensions. Qualify under both counts: pension savings are tax deductible, pension funds grow free of income and capital gains tax. Within the prescribed limits, make sure you are putting in adequate amounts into your pension. With very few exceptions, most people could do with more pension savings than they have already. Advice rating:★★.

2. Business Expansion Schemes (BES) - See Chapter Five. An investment of up to £40,000 may be made each year into shares of 'qualifying' companies which are, broadly speaking, new trading companies not quoted on any stock exchange. Income tax relief is available against the cost of the shares, but will be withdrawn if the shares are sold within five years. After that time, profits made on a sale are also exempt from capital gains tax on their first disposal. BES investments can be risky: do seek professional advice. Advice rating:★★★

Also in this category come trusts investing in property located in Enterprise Zones. Here, there is no limit to the investment, but it must be held as long as twenty-five years to avoid the possibility of income tax relief clawback. Advice rating: ★★★.

3. Personal Equity Plans. No tax relief is available on investment here, sadly, but a maximum of £3,000 may be invested in UK shares and to a limited extent in unit trusts free of income and capital gains tax - so long as you don't touch it for the year following the one in which the investment is made. Advice rating: ★★.

4. National Savings Certificates. Interest that is free of all taxes is the carrot here: not tempting for non-taxpayers and rarely for basic-raters, it can be very valuable for higher rate payers and for those caught in the 'age allowance trap'. Premium bond winnings are also tax-free if you like a gamble. Advice rating: ★.

5. Investment Bonds. These are not a particularly tax efficient investment for the average investor – see Chapter Five for details. However, they include a facility whereby holders can withdraw up to 5 per cent a year of their original investment tax-free for up to twenty years. Can be good for higher rate taxpayers looking for income, or for those caught in the 'age allowance trap'. Advice rating: ★★.

Tax and Perks

Unless you are earning less than £8,500 a year, many of the common 'fringe benefits' offered by employers attract tax. But there are important exceptions, and someone who is self-employed is entitled to look enviously at the employee enjoying paid holidays, pension contributions, sick pay and life assurance schemes, and cheap meals in the company canteen – all of which are undoubtedly benefits of employment and are tax-free as far as the lucky employee is concerned.

The most famous – or infamous – tax-free perk for the employee is the luncheon voucher. When its value was first set, it could buy a good three-course meal; today, the 15 pence limit might go some of the way towards a cup of tea. Better by far for employees to press for improvements in the other tax-free perks mentioned above than to try to persuade the Inland Revenue to increase the limit on LVs: every year there is a campaign, and every year it fails.

Clothing bought by the employer which is specifically required for your work can be tax-free, but the definition is curious. Overalls count: a dark business suit does not, even if you argue that such a suit is only ever used for work.

Certain low or interest-free loans can also qualify as a tax-free perk. The rule here is that the value of the loan must not exceed £200 a year, and the value is worked out by reference to the Official Rate of Interest which the Revenue announces from time to time. The value is the difference between the amount (if any) of interest you actually pay, and the amount it would have cost using the official rate. This could be quite useful: the £200 limit would provide the wherewithal to buy many an annual season ticket.

Table 2
Tax and the Company Car

Original market value	Scale benefits		Fuel benefits
	Cars under 4 years old	Cars over 4 years old	
Up to £19,250			
Up to 1400cc	£1,050	£700	£480
1400 to 2000cc	£1,400	£940	£600
2001cc and over	£2,200	£1,450	£900
£19,251 to £29,000	£2,900	£1,940	£900
£29,001 and over	£4,600	3,060	£900

If you are earning more than £8,500 a year, or if you are a director of a company no matter what your earnings, many other perks will be taxable. They can still be worthwhile, however. Top of the list for many is the company car.

Cars are taxed according to their age and the size of their engine, unless they were extremely expensive when new, in which case their price determines the charge. Table 2 gives details. If your employer also pays for petrol which you use for private motoring, you must pay tax on this as well, as shown in the third column.

There is scope for minimising your tax charge by choosing a car with a smaller engine, or by reimbursing your employer for any petrol he gives you if its value is small. The biggest saving, however, is by clocking up the business miles a year. Drive less than the minimum, and the scale is upped by 50 per cent: drive more than the maximum and you are rewarded by a 50 per cent decrease.

Employee share schemes can also be a good way of rewarding a workforce: the key here is that the scheme must be specifically approved by the Inland Revenue. There are several variations on the theme: a share option scheme gives the employee the right to buy shares in his employer's company at a date sometime in the future, but at today's price. Assuming the share price goes up in the meantime, the employee could make an instant profit by re-selling – and he would be liable to capital gains tax (if any) not income tax, assuming all the regulations had been properly obeyed.

Are perks a good idea?

Whether taxable or tax-free, the answer generally has to be 'yes', but there is a limit. Most people prefer to choose how to spend their remuneration, rather than having to take it from the company store. And the extent of many of the financial perks offered by companies - notably pensions and life assurance, but also redundancy money - is fixed by reference to the money you actually earn, excluding the value of the extras.

Further Information
In addition to the books mentioned above, there is *The Touche Ross Tax Guide to Pay and Perks 1987-8* by Bill Packer and Elaine Baker, published by Papermac, price £4.95.

Capital Gains Tax
Capital Gains Tax (CGT) is, to be frank, a pig's ear of a tax, and much wishful thinking (I suspect on both sides of the Revenue fence) has gone into the expectation of it being abolished. CGT remains to torment us for at least another year, however, so we might as well get to grips with it.

The principle is simple: that you should be taxed on any profits you make from selling something, or 'disposing of an asset' as the jargon goes. A few things are exempt from the tax altogether. They include first and foremost your own home; private motor cars; National Savings Certificates and gilts, and 'tangible movable property' with an expected life of less than fifty years, such as boats or animals. The other side of the coin, however, is that any losses you make in selling these items cannot be offset against gains made elsewhere. The rate at which gains are charged is the same as your marginal rate of income tax, in other words 25 per cent or 40 per cent. Perhaps the most important provision is the *annual exemption*: gains of £5,000 in the current tax year are entirely free of tax. Everyone is entitled to this exemption although married couples currently have to make do with one between them.

Where tax is charged, it is only on 'net gains', ie after deducting any capital losses you may have made during the tax year as well. What makes the tax such a bugbear, however, is the indexation provisions. Some years ago, 1982 to be precise, the Government decided that it was unfair to tax gains which might be no more than inflation-only profits. So an indexation allowance was brought in, which allows you to increase the purchase price of the asset (and if appropriate any expenses incurred in purchasing it) by the amount of inflation we have had since the month you bought it. Only then is any profit, over and above inflation, liable for the tax.

This indexation allowance can also be used to inflate any

TAX AND TAX PLANNING

capital losses you may have made, and so enlarge the amount of tax-free gains you can make in that year.

It is the indexation allowance that can prove fiendishly difficult to work out. The Revenue publishes a table each month showing the progress of the Retail Price Index, allowing you to work out what allowance you are entitled to.

If your gain is from a single asset bought in one go, it can be awkward enough: but suppose you have built up a holding in a unit trust by means of a monthly savings scheme over several years? There is, strictly speaking, no alternative to doing indexation sums separately for every single monthly payment you have made.

Some investors lose patience and throw the whole lot at their tax office, asking them to sort it out; the informal word from the Revenue is that you might be lucky and find an official who is willing to carry out the arithmetic for you, but you might not. He would be entitled to issue an estimated assessment on you - and the ball would be back in your court if you wished to disprove it.

The one silver lining to this cloud of indexation is that any gains made prior to 1982 are now completely exempt from the tax, whether they are 'genuine' or 'inflation-only' gains. This measure is irrelevant, obviously, to those who have only recently acquired investments, but should be a help to people who have been investing for many years.

Remember that the annual exemption applies only to gains (less losses) that you have realised in a particular tax year. If you are nudging the top of the band with your profits, it can be worth selling your investments just before the end of the tax year (even if you intend to repurchase them shortly afterwards) to 'crystallise' that gain.

If you know you are going to have to pay the tax, a bit of expert timing can help. Capital gains tax for profits made in (say) the 1987-8 year is payable on 1 December 1988. So by delaying any sale until just *after* the 5th of April in any year, you can, at least, delay the evil hour of payment by up to almost a year.

Information
The Inland Revenue issue several free leaflets on CGT, including CGT4: Capital Gains Tax and owner occupied

houses; CGT8: Capital Gains Tax; and CGT13: The indexation allowance for quoted shares.

CGT and Investment

Despite its complications, it is clear that CGT is a (relatively) nice tax. Few investors succeed in realising net gains in excess of the tax-free limit each year, and the 1987 crash has undoubtedly 'helped' those who might otherwise have been in danger.

The reverse side of the coin is that, almost without exception, making capital gains involves taking risks. There are exceptions: notably low coupon and index-linked gilts. With low coupon gilts, the price is usually at a considerable discount to the value at which the gilt will be redeemed by the Government at maturity. In the meantime, the level of interest an investor receives is also low, but higher rate taxpayers are not likely to be too much worried by this. Index-linked gilts are also, for tax purposes, similar to low coupons. In both cases, the bulk of the reward stored up for the investor comes in the shape of capital gains, not income. And the icing on the cake here is that gains made from an investment in gilts are specifically exempted from capital gains tax.

Just about all other investments which are capable of producing capital gains carry some degree of risk; and while, with the £5,000 exemption and the indexation provisions, the tax system gives a gentle nudge in favour of capital gains, you should never let the tax tail wag the investment dog. You should decide what sort of investments you want first - and then think about their tax implications.

But beware. There are some oddities in the tax system which may mislead you. Investments such as shares, unit trusts and investment trusts all fall under the CGT regime, so you can benefit directly from the tax-free limit. Not so with insurance policies, whether they are regular savings schemes or single premium bond funds. These policies are often marketed as 'tax-free' or (slightly less misleadingly) 'tax-free to the investor'.

It is true that the investor does not usually have to pay any extra tax personally (but see Chapter Five on bonds and the higher rate taxpayer); but that is because the tax has been paid already, by the life company on his behalf! And you can be sure the life company does not find the means to do so from its own pocket, but deducts the appropriate amount from your fund. And it cannot use your 'personal' CGT yearly allowance.

Time and again, this fact catches investors out: with most insurance policies the deduction is 'invisible' so perhaps investors are not always aware of what they are missing. With a few old-style policies, however, the deduction for CGT is shown in black and white on the statement issued when the policy matures.

The moral of this tale is simple. If you have decided to invest in equities for their capital growth prospects, and you want a pooled investment vehicle, then you should consider a unit or investment trust, where you can make use of your personal exemption, and avoid the life assurance fund.

Pensions are a paragon of tax efficient virtue as regards CGT, no less than income tax. The pension tax fund pays no CGT on any gains it makes, and nor do you when you start receiving the pension, even if you opt to take out a portion of it as a lump sum.

PEPs are also goody-goodies for CGT purposes as any profits made here are exempt without limit, assuming you hold the plan for the requisite amount of time. It may take some years (and some luck) to get your maximum annual investment of £3,000 up to a figure where CGT threatens, but if you do, it's nice to know there is no question of paying the tax.

Inheritance Tax

Inheritance tax is the tax payable on money or assets that you give away to others – either during your lifetime or after death. The main rules are as follows:

Most gifts, with some important exceptions, are potentially liable to Inheritance Tax (IHT), whether they are made during life or after death. Gifts made during lifetime are treated less harshly than those made on death.

The main exceptions, where gifts can be made without giving rise to even the possibility of IHT are as follows:

1. Any gifts made between husband and wife.
2. Gifts of up to £3,000 a year.
3. 'Small gifts' of not more than £250 per recipient each year.
4. Gifts that form normal expenditure out of income: to qualify for this, donors should be able to demonstrate that their normal standard of living is not affected by the gifts.

5. Gifts in consideration of marriage – £5,000 from each parent and £2,500 from each grandparent.
6. Gifts to charities.

Gifts that qualify under any of the above headings are totally exempt. Nearly all other gifts made during lifetime are *potentially* exempt. Potentially exempt transfers (universally known as Pets for short) do not give rise to any IHT at the time they are made, but if the donor dies within seven years, they become up for grabs along with the rest of the donor's estate. However, as long as he has survived for at least three years after making the gift, a 'taper' relief applies on the amount of that gift, as the table below shows.

Years between time of gift and death	% of full rate payable
up to 3 years	100
3 to 4 years	80
4 to 5 years	60
5 to 6 years	40
6 to 7 years	20

The full rates of IHT depend on whether the gift is made during life, or after death, as Table 1 shows. The 'lifetime' rate is not very important as most gifts fall under the heading of 'potentially exempt' – it is only gifts to, for example, certain types of trust which attract IHT immediately.

Inheritance Tax and Financial Planning

As you can see from Table 1, there is a substantial 'nil rate band' – in the 1988-9 tax year of £110,000 – which people can give away without any IHT being payable. So in theory the answer to IHT planning is simple; give away all your assets barring £110,000 during your lifetime, make sure you live another seven years, and you're home and dry.

The problem is, of course, that life simply doesn't work like that. The very rich might be able to contemplate giving away substantial chunks of their assets during their lives – most of us can't, not least because a good proportion of anyone's estate is likely to be their house, and it would be somewhat inconvenient to have to give that away while we're still alive.

The rules on IHT are very strict on what are termed 'gifts with reservation'. As far as IHT is concerned, 'gifts with reservation' are not true gifts at all. You can't, for example,

give away your house to your children but reserve the right
to live in it till the end of your days and hope to escape IHT
in this way. Even if you do without a legal agreement, or any
written document, the Revenue might decide that there was
an 'unwritten agreement' that you could stay in the house.
As with many aspects of tax, the precise circumstances in
which some transaction takes place will dictate whether or
not you are liable to tax, and this is often something only
established by case law.

Even if you do have substantial assets which are not tied up
in your home, you may have good reason why you don't want
to give them away; you may need the income they produce
to live on, or you may be unwilling to hand over large sums
to children or grandchildren who (whatever their age) have
not, in your opinion, reached the years of discretion.

Any sensible tax planning, in other words, has to be within
reason - *your* reason. All other things being equal, however,
you should consider the following moves:

1. If you are married, try to make sure that your joint assets
are divided equally between the two of you, so that when
the first partner dies, his/her share can be left at least partly
to the next generation, making use of the nil rate band.

2. Make as much use as you can of the annual exemptions,
in particular the £3,000 exemption and the 'gifts made out of
income' provision.

3. If you have considerable assets, try to use the nil rate
band during your lifetime (and make sure you live another
seven years!) so the potentially exempt transfer becomes
fully exempt.

4. With life assurance and pension policies, it is possible to
arrange these in such a way that any sum payable on death is
outside your estate for IHT purposes. If there is likely to be
a large IHT bill to be faced on your death, you could start
a life assurance policy specifically to provide the funds to
pay that bill. This is a particularly useful ploy, because you
could almost certainly argue that the premiums you pay for
this count as 'normal expenditure out of your income' and
so exempt from IHT.

5. If you don't wish to give money away outright, there are
certain types of trust which can be suitable. You will probably
need to have quite substantial assets to make the exercise worthwhile, and you would certainly need professional advice.

6. If you are retired and are considering a Home Income Plan (see Chapter Nine) you should remember that this can have positively beneficial effects for IHT; by taking out an interest–only mortgage on your property (which is what such a plan involves) you are decreasing its value for IHT purposes as the capital has to be repaid after your death.

A word about tax planning in general

Tax planning is all very well, but it does have to be kept in its rightful place. Some investors, in their desire to avoid paying tax, have lost all their money by depositing their cash in some dodgy offshore bank. I'm certainly not suggesting they deserved it, but it can sometimes appear that normal considerations of prudence fly out of the window when a promise of 'tax-free investment' is made. Such people, anyway, are under a misapprehension: as a general rule, anyone who lives in this country is liable to tax on his income, wherever it arises.

As far as complicated tax planning schemes are concerned, you should recognise that, in the end, the Revenue has the whip hand. Do you remember Gladstone from *1066 and All That*?

He spent his declining years 'trying to guess the answer to the Irish Question. Unfortunately, whenever he was getting warm, the Irish secretly changed the Question'. In much the same way, however carefully the tax planners devise complicated schemes to avoid tax, the Government and the Revenue can always change the rules.

Diana Wright

Inheritance Tax: Further Information
IHT1: Inheritance tax – free leaflet from the Inland Revenue.
Inheritance Tax: Your Opportunity by Amyas Morse. Published by Deloitte Haskins & Sells, price £4.95.

11 The Regulatory Maze

For a nation steeped in traditions of Empire and financial supremacy, Britain imposed on its investment industry remarkably little red tape. None at all, in fact, in certain areas - until this year. The only paperwork required, for example, to set up in business as an independent investment adviser was of the headed variety and, if you wanted to damn the expense, some embossed business cards. Unlike solicitors, doctors or accountants, so-called investment professionals needed to pass no examinations or attain any authorisation. Standards were self-imposed, if imposed at all, with the result that scandals of incompetence and fraud surfaced monotonously.

Of course, within the institutions, as opposed to one-man bands, standards and regulations had grown with London's eminence as a financial centre. Membership of the Stock Exchange was won through examination; compensation schemes were run by the Exchange and the Building Societies Association; the Department of Trade and Industry oversaw insurance companies, unit trusts, and those securities dealers who did not operate through the Stock Exchange; the Old Lady of Threadneedle Street peered over her horned rims at the banks; and the Prevention of Fraud (Investments) Act was supposed to fall heavily on transgressors.

But these measures evolved and operated independently and unequally; no coherent structure regulated the financial world. For Mrs Thatcher's new age of privatisation and popular capitalism to flourish, order and protection were vital for all investors.

So back in July 1981 the then Secretary of State for Trade, John Biffen, commissioned pipe-smoking Professor L.C.B. 'Jim' Gower to conduct a review of investor protection. Gower's report in 1984 metamorphosed into the Financial Services Bill, which became an Act last year, which came into force this April. It is primarily aimed at giving you, the individual investor, a fair deal for your money. How? Like this:

The Securities and Investments Board

The slow boat to investor protection finally beached at a system of self-regulation encased within a statutory framework. Since 29 April 1988 it has been a criminal offence under the Financial Services Act (FSA) for anyone to carry on 'investment business' without being properly authorised. In turn that authorisation entails compliance with comprehensive rules set up and administered by bodies within the industry itself.

These rules are no mere mass of technical verbiage - they perceptibly affect the way bank managers, insurance salesmen and the like deal with their customers.

What is 'investment business'? The FSA covers all people and businesses dealing in, advising on or managing investments, operating unit trusts, and arranging dealing in investments. The definition of 'investments' includes shares, gilts, options, futures and long-term insurance contracts such as the endowment policies often linked to mortgages.

The FSA does not cover, among other things, 'dealings as principal' - ie where individuals or companies buy or sell investments on their own behalf; investment advice given in the course of non-investment business; and investment advice given in newspapers. Lloyd's insurance market is another, conspicuous, exemption despite a rash of scandals over misconduct in recent years.

The distinctions are complex but two simple examples give their flavour. Buying a motor insurance policy is not directly affected; such straightforward insurance is not classed as an investment. But buying a pension policy is, after the FSA, subject to strict new regulations. Similarly, an individual filling in a newspaper coupon to buy unit trusts on his own behalf is in no different position than before; but a professional intermediary offering advice on unit trusts to the public has now to adhere to new standards and practices.

To understand the impact of the regulations it is first necessary to grasp who will administer them. At the top of the pile (see *figure 1*) remains the Secretary of State at the Department of Trade and Industry; but beneath has been created a new body called the Securities and Investments Board (SIB) to which most powers of authorisation and regulation have been delegated.

The SIB is responsible for the vetting and authorisation

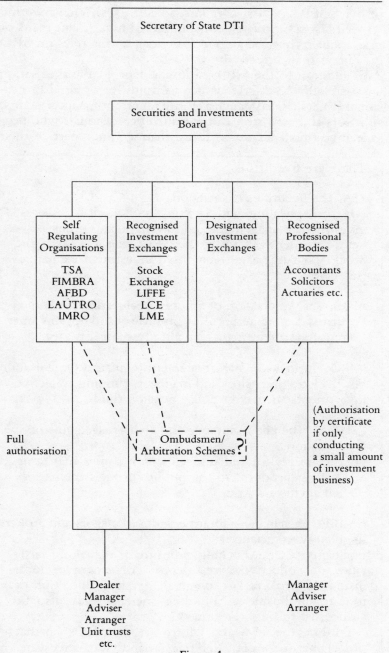

Figure 1

of five Self Regulatory Organisations (SROs), each covering a specific area of investment. Individual investment firms or practitioners must be authorised either by the relevant SRO or, failing that, directly by the SIB.

In addition to the SROs, a lower degree of authorisation is possible by certificates issued through Recognised Professional Bodies (RPBs), such as those representing accountants, solicitors and actuaries. But any such professionals who provide investment advice as more than a minor part of their

---

There are five SROs:

TSA. The Securities Association
For firms dealing and broking in securities, shares, investment management and international money market instruments. This is the SRO that fits with the Stock Exchange as a 'recognised investment exchange' (see below).

AFBD. The Association of Futures Dealers and Brokers
For firms dealing and broking in futures and options and giving investment management advice in this area.

IMRO. The Investment Management Regulatory Organisation
For the likes of trustees and managers running collective investments such as in-house pension funds.

LAUTRO. The Life Assurance and Unit Trust Regulatory Organisation
For life insurance and unit trust companies managing and selling products to the public through themselves or tied agents.

FIMBRA. The Financial Intermediaries Managers and Brokers Regulatory Association
For firms dealing, broking, advising or managing securities or collective investments. For example, local insurance brokers or solicitors (if they do a lot of investment business). Building societies may also be authorised through Fimbra.

Fimbra, the TSA and Lautro are the SROs (in that order) likely to be of most interest to individual investors.

business are likely to have to be fully authorised by an SRO.

The SROs are, if you like, the club committees; the FSA also defines the playing fields. Recognised Investment Exchanges (RIEs) will include the Stock Exchange, the London International Financial Futures Exchange, the London Metal Exchange, and the London Commodities Exchange. These all have their own regulations on reporting trading. Investment games played outside the RIEs will be possible, but only subject to strict rules on reporting trading directly to the SIB.

Overseas stock exchanges and the like that the SIB deems fit and proper are called Designated Investment Exchanges. Any overseas investment exchange without a permanent base in the UK which wants UK residents to deal in its instruments must apply to the SIB for designation. Overseas exchanges with permanent bases in the UK must be authorised in the normal way.

For the man or woman in the Clapham Mini Metro the key point in this morass of acronyms is that any investment adviser must be authorised. This will be apparent on their notepaper and can be checked through the SIB or SROs or RPBs. Anyone carrying on 'investment business' who is not authorised is a crook.

What Authorisation Means for Investor Protection

Sticking a fake burglar alarm on the wall of your house may deter the opportunistic thief but not the habitual; only alarms that are switched on then carry weight. Quite how switched on are the SROs will only be revealed by their practice. But the theory is that they will have a two-pronged attack: weeding out the baddies at the start and keeping an eye on those firms which are authorised to operate.

First, applications for authorisation by an SRO will require detailed information on the directors or partners of an investment business, and its financial status. Individuals will have to be fit and proper persons, firms will have to meet certain financial minima in terms of capital.

Secondly, authorised firms will have to follow the 'conduct of business rules'. These lay down detailed procedures aimed at ensuring honest and fair practice, and the maintenance of records to prove it. Some key points are:

★Before dealing for individuals, firms must provide a written customer agreement. This should make clear how you are allowing the firm to act on your behalf.

★Advice must be suitable to an individual's circumstances.

★Deals must be done at the best price available.

★Products recommended must be the best in their field.

★Individuals or firms selling life insurance and unit trusts must make it clear whether they are acting as independent intermediaries (giving best advice from the whole market) or appointed representatives selling solely the products of their own company. This concept is called polarisation.

★Clients' money must be held in separate bank accounts and proper accounting records kept. Firms' accounts must be audited, and their SROs informed if the audits are qualified in any way.

★Dealing in clients' investments purely to generate commission – a practice known as 'churning' – is prohibited.

★Cold calling is restricted.

★Records must be kept to show how the rules have been followed and how any complaints have been handled.

The SIB and SROs will have the power to conduct spot checks – if necessary entering premises to examine all records. Of course, much depends on the interpretation of phrases like 'best advice' and 'best execution'. But though it is virtually impossible to give positive definitions, the regulators feel confident that they will be able to ascertain what is *not* 'best' – and punish malpractors accordingly.

For example, if you go to an insurance intermediary for a pension policy and he or she sells you one from Joe Bloggs Insurance Ltd, it may be arguable whether that was best available or not. But if it is demonstrably worse than several others on the market or it turns out to be Pet Insurance covering veterinary fees, he or she clearly has not followed the conduct of business rules.

The concepts of 'best advice', 'best execution' and others, are aimed at ensuring investors receive an acceptable standard of service – in a similar way that trading standards are imposed on the sale of goods. They do not and should not, however, provide any blanket guarantee. The game must be played by the rules, but the risks of injury, winning, losing – even being rained off – remain. Interest rates and the value of shares can go down as well as up, and the rules offer no specious protection against that.

Polarisation

The furore that raged over whether polarisation should be introduced or not testifies to how radical a change it is. The principle is simple: financial advisers should make it plain to clients in what capacity they act. Are they offering independent advice on products drawn from the whole market place or simply recommending products from one or two companies with whom they have a particularly chummy (ie lucrative) commission arrangement?

Take a novice investor who decides the time has come to settle down and buy some unit trusts. Until this year, if he contacted a bank or insurance company's financial planning department there was no requirement for either adviser to reveal whether the trust they recommended – out of the 1000 – plus in existence – was connected with their company or not. Self-interest, which often conflicts with the customer's interest, could easily be disguised. For example, the names of many unit trusts do not betray their company of origin. If a financial adviser said 'I recommend x', it was difficult for the uninitiated to know whether they should reply 'Well, you would say that, wouldn't you'.

With polarisation, however, advisers will have to state on their stationery and business cards whether they act purely for one company (as an 'appointed' or 'company representative') or whether they deal with the whole market (as 'independent intermediaries').

Bank and building society branches will have to choose one or other route. If they opt for independence they will not be able to recommend their own products; if they opt to be 'company representatives' they will be able to sell only their own products or those of a single company with which they have linked.

In the gentlemanly discussions preceding the final rules, the banks used their muscle to win a concession that they could make their branches company representatives, but also operate subsidiary companies as independent intermediaries. They want to have their cake and sell it. But the rules on communication between tied branch and independent subsidiary should still mean the investor is clear about the status and prejudice of his advisers.

Of the ten largest building societies only Abbey National has chosen to make its branches appointed representatives (of the insurance company Friends Provident). Of the big four banks only National Westminster has chosen to make its branches independent advisers. The Law Society has decided that solicitors conducting investment business must act as independent intermediaries.

How to Complain and Get Your Money Back

Light will shine through the grey areas only in time as individual complaints establish precedents. The first course of action if you become an aggrieved investor will be to approach the individual adviser or firm concerned. Remember, a firm's records should be able to demonstrate that you have received 'best advice'. That is, a product suited to your needs and, if from an independent intermediary, from among the best performing companies in the field.

If initial enquiries fail to produce results, the next port of call is either the relevant SRO or the SIB itself. The sheer legwork and administration involved in an investigation makes the SRO a better choice - Fimbra, for example, intends to have in the region of 100 inspectors, while the total staff of the SIB is currently little more than that.

If a breach of the rules has occurred, the SRO could threaten the firm with expulsion - which would force it to stop trading - unless it made restitution.

On a different tack, Section 62 of the FSA specifically enables investors to sue firms if they have lost money because the rules of authorisation have not been followed. Potentially this means that if investors can prove they have not received, say, 'best advice' they could recover any money they had lost as a result. Section 62 to all those fully authorised with an SRO only applies from 3 October 1988; however, it is already in operation for investment businesses authorised directly by the SIB or those with 'interim authorisation'. (The latter status was granted to businesses that applied for authorisation to an SRO before the end of February but whose applications have yet to be processed.)

What happens if an investment firm goes bust and cannot pay its creditors? A compensation scheme, funded by all members of the SROs, will operate from August 1988 in most of the industry. If an authorised firm goes into liquidation and an investor is awarded compensation, he will be covered for 100 per cent of investments up to £30,000 and 90 per cent of a further £20,000 - ie a ceiling of £48,000. The key point here is that the compensation scheme only pays out when an authorised firm goes into liquidation - not before. If a firm has not been authorised in the first place its contracts are not enforceable; investors can take legal action, civil or criminal, to recover their funds. However, this is usually an expensive and lengthy procedure, with no guarantee that investors will recover their money even if they win their case. The compensation scheme will not cover unauthorised firms.

Obviously prevention is better than cure - always check that an investment adviser or firm is properly authorised before parting with any hard-earned lucre.

The Men/Women in White Coats

There are other avenues of appeal if the various branches of the FSA prove fruitless.

An Ombudsman (an office that dates back to 1809 in Sweden, but only some twenty years in the UK) is supposed to act as an impartial umpire in disputes between members of the public and institutions. A few already exist in sectors of the financial services industry. Participants in these schemes agree that disputes of certain types and up to certain financial limits (they vary between different ombudsmen) can be taken to an ombudsman whose decision may be either binding on both parties or only a recommendation that does not preclude further legal action.

It is not possible here to list the different parameters within which various ombudsmen operate. But generally speaking they should not be the first recourse in a complaint. As an aggrieved investor you should approach the firm concerned first, not only because it may be willing to rectify any error, but also because the ombudsmen are understaffed (and that's an understatement).

However, ombudsmen do already operate for insurance companies, banks, and building societies; and the legal profession has the Solicitors Complaints Bureau. (A list of useful addresses can be found at the end of this chapter.)

The SIB has the power to require that all SROs and RPBs have effective measures for dealing with disputes, but does not have the power to institute an ombudsman scheme throughout the investment industry (as it had once hoped). However, some of the SROs are considering instituting their own ombudsmen.

Newspapers are supposed to be impartial crusaders after truth, too, which entices many irate investors to send their complaints to the financial editors of *The Sunday Times* and other, perhaps less well known, organs. I know this because if there is one subject that personal finance journalists get emotional about more than any other, it is the sack loads of readers' letters that regularly demolish their desks. Now the pen is mightier than the sword, but the printing press mightier than the pen. You may write complaining in the most surgical terms to, say, your bank manager – all in vain. Only fear that the rest of the nation may read about the bank's incompetence will, shall we say, melt hearts in high places and restore the £1.95 levied because you went overdrawn for one day when the bank failed to credit a cheque to your account promptly.

But, like the ombudsmen, personal finance journalists have only so many hands (and can usually only type with two fingers). It must be said that the chances of a letter of complaint being taken up and resolved are slim, though I would not wish to deter people from writing in – it is an invaluable source of information about what is happening out there. But it is worth taking a few simple measures to increase the chances of action following.

First, write or preferably type legibly; give full details (journalists are not clairvoyants), but do so concisely; only send photocopies of relevant documents, no originals; and be as precise as possible.

Choosing An Adviser

It is one of the ironies of regulation that the FSA will achieve its aim if the principal bodies it creates – the SIB and SROs – do not become casualty wards for injured investors. Far better that the rules beget worthy advisers in the first place than the machinery of enforcement be called upon to punish transgressors. So, the 64,000 dollar question, how do you select a suitable financial adviser? One way to achieve this is to make some basic decisions yourself first. Try to define what sort of advice you are seeking.

For example, if you want to minimise tax or arrange a

will, a tax accountant or solicitor will be appropriate. The Law Society or Institute of Chartered Accountants would be starting points.

If you have spare cash and no investments, you need general financial advice; the investment department of a bank or an independent intermediary would be appropriate. Fimbra would be one way of finding an independent intermediary.

If you have your house and pension under control and still have spare cash to invest, an independent intermediary or a stockbroker might be appropriate. The Securities Association would be a source for a stockbroker.

If you are happy with the service and performance of a financial company you already deal with, its company representative might be appropriate.

Of course, these are not hard and fast recommendations and much depends on individual firms' expertise. But they help to narrow down the choices initially.

What the FSA has made concrete is the status of advisers and, in some cases, what they are earning from your business. First check that investment advisers are authorised (either themselves or their company) by an SRO. Then establish whether they are an independent intermediary or a company representative.

The rules, which are the subject of much argument, at present decree the following: independents, giving unbiased advice drawn from the whole market, must disclose what commission they will earn on the sale of any life insurance or unit trust product. In the buying and selling of shares, stockbrokers and banks already declare the commission or charges they make.

Appointed representatives will sell only their own or appointed company's products, though they are obliged to recommend the most suitable ones within their range for your needs. They will not be required to disclose the commission they earn.

On balance the independent intermediary holds the aces: he is not peddling a company line but should select products from among the best according to the latest information. The question is, how competent is he or she?

The fact that they are authorised should be some reassurance. Beyond that, judgements must be made as with any business: the quality of staff, premises, administration and the look in their eye. Pay particular attention to how they handle clients' money – it must be held in bank accounts separate to those of their own. Ask questions: have they been established long? what previous experience do they have? any relevant qualifications? do they keep in regular contact with clients – perhaps through a newsletter? Make sure, too, that they ask you questions. One of the effects of the FSA is that advisers must 'know their client' – ie build up a proper picture of their financial affairs so that they can be suitably advised.

No Panaceas Here

With all the ballyhoo and bugle blowing in the financial world from Big Bang and the Financial Services Act, it is important to remember the limitations of investor protection. First, not all the FSA's elements apply from April 29. In some circumstances the compensation scheme, suing under Section 62, the need for customer agreements, declaring authorisation on business notepaper, and some requirements for capital adequacy for investment firms have been delayed until later in 1988 or even until early 1989. Second, the FSA and its compensation scheme cover 'investment business' – that leaves plenty of financial matters beyond its scope. This is perhaps where the ombudsmen come into their own, dealing with, say, complaints about non-investment insurance policies.

Remember, too, that if you place your money with Shark Brothers Bank in an obscure unrecognised offshore financial centre, you won't have the protection of the FSA. So, too, if a silver-tongued salesman telephones from Switzerland with an unbelievably good share offer, Fimbra will have no power to retrieve your cheque from being spent on the ski slopes.

Offshore financial centres, such as the Isle of Man and the Channel Islands which bask in sunny tax climes, can apply to the DTI for recognition as 'designated territories'. To win designation they need to demonstrate equivalent investor protection rules to those of the FSA. Designation will allow them to market their products to the 'onshore' public. Without designation, their products cannot be marketed to the public, but can be channelled through investment professionals, who will face the rigour of the FSA here.

But to put it simply, whatever the regulations, unravelling a dispute that originates overseas is going to be more difficult and more expensive than one closer to home.

Remember, too, that many financial advisers earn their living largely by commission. This causes two problems: 1) they may be biased because they earn more commission from some products than others 2) they may be biased because if they don't sell at least some product or other (even if you don't really need it) they don't make money.

The first of these problems is being smoothed out; the second will remain, despite the FSA, unless advisers operate on the basis of charging fees for consultations and services, rather than taking commissions for sales.

No matter whether statutory or self-imposed regulation stands all financial advisers inside man-traps strapped into straitjackets tied up in red tape, there is one rule that will always - and rightly - remain: *caveat emptor* (let the buyer beware).

As Professor Jim Gower pithily said in his report: the extension of financial regulation 'should not be greater than is needed adequately to protect investors and this, emphatically does *not* mean it should seek to achieve the impossible task of protecting fools from their own folly. All it should do is to try to prevent people being made fools of.'

Richard Woods

Information and Contacts

The Securities and Investments Board
3 Royal Exchange Buildings
London EC3V 3NL
01-283 2474

Financial Intermediaries Managers and Brokers Regulatory Organisation
22 Great Tower Street
London EC3R 5AQ
01-929 2711

The Securities Association
The Stock Exchange Building
Old Broad Street
London EC2N 1EQ
01-256 9000

Life Insurance and Unit Trust Regulatory Organisation
Centre Point
103 New Oxford Street
London WC1A 1PT
01-379 0444

Association of Futures Brokers and Dealers
Plantation House
4-16 Mincing Lane
London EC3N 3DX
01-626 9763

Investment Management Regulatory Organisation
Centre Point
103 New Oxford Street
London WC1A 1PT
01-379 0444

Insurance Ombudsman
31 Southampton Row
London WC1B 5HJ
01-242 8613

Banking Ombudsman
Citadel House
5-11 Fetter Lane
London EC4A 1BR
01-583 1395

Building Societies Ombudsman
Grosvenor Gardens House
35-37 Grosvenor Gardens
London SW1
01-931 0044

Solicitors Complaints Bureau
Portland House
Stag Place
London SW1E 5BL
01-834 2288

The Law Society
113 Chancery Lane
London WC2A 1P1
01-242 1222

Institute of Chartered Accountants in England and Wales
Chartered Accountants Hall
Moorgate Place
London EC2
01-628 7060

The Department of Trade and Industry
1-19 Victoria Street
London SW1
01-215 7877

Index